THE SOCIAL MEDIA SURVIVAL GUIDE FOR NONPROFITS AND CHARITABLE ORGANIZATIONS:

How to Build Your Base of Support and Fast-Track Your Fundraising Efforts Using Social Media

Sherrie A. Madia, Ph.D.

Full Court Press

Full Court Press
A Division of Base Camp Communications, LLC
P.O. Box 148
Voorhees, NJ 08043

Find Us Online:
SocialMediaForNonprofitsBook.com

Library of Congress Cataloging-in-Publication Data
Madia, Sherrie Ann.
The Social Media Survival Guide for Nonprofits and Charitable Organizations / by Sherrie Madia.

Summary: How to employ social media tactics to enhance all aspects of fundraising in the not-for-profit sector—from cultivation, to engagement, to fundraising and stewardship.

p. cm.

ISBN: 978-0-9826185-9-2

2011920913

Printed in the United States of America

10 9 8 7 6 5 4 3 2 1 First Edition

CONTENTS

FOREWORD   *vii*

ACKNOWLEDGMENTS   *x*

INTRODUCTION   *xi*

CHAPTER 1. The Online State of Nonprofits and Charitable Organizations   1
 A Pervasive Medium   4
 Social Media in Action   5
 What Your Nonprofit Can Do With Social Media   8

CHAPTER 2. Your Organization and the New Media Landscape   17
 Social Media for Nonprofits: Risk vs. Reward   17
 The Risks   18
 Avoidance Rationale   24
 Why Every Organization Must Engage in Social Media   27
 The Rewards   30

CHAPTER 3. Assess Your Online Presence   37
 Stepping Into the Social Media Space: Your Web 2.0 Presence   37
 What Is Web 2.0?   39
 Sharing Your Organization's Story   43
 Core Message Points   43
 Organizational Commitment   47
 Resource Audit   49

CHAPTER 4. A New Kind of Prospect Research   53
 Locating Your Donor Base   54
 Your Social Media Pipeline   55
 Custom Communities   61
 Metrics Old and New   62

CHAPTER 5. Fundraising Toolkit   65
 Nonprofit Facebook Fans   65
 Tweet Your Core Messages   71
 Link Up to LinkedIn   75
 Your Charitable Organization in the Blogosphere   77
 Engage Through Flickr   81
 Position with Podcasts   84
 YouTube: The New "Must Have"   87
 Video-Chat Touch Points   89
 Going Mobile   91

CHAPTER 6. Today's Ideal Fundraiser 97

    How to Use Social Media to Your Advantage 99

    Social Media Is a Branding Tool 105

    The Importance of Online Cultivation 106

    Ways to Use Social Media to Get More People on Board 107

    Choose Your Networks Wisely 108

    More Social Media Best Practices 109

CHAPTER 7. Strategies of Engagement 113

    Ways to Put Social Networks to Work for the Cause 115

    Capturing New Audiences 118

    Broaden Your Organizational Reach 120

    How to Connect the Social Media Dots 122

CHAPTER 8. Communications 127

    Your Social Media Case Statement 127

    Social Media Integration 128

    Email and E-newsletters 129

    Peer-to-Peer Appeals 133

    Annual Reports 135

    The Social Media Ask 138

CHAPTER 9. Special Events 143

    Incorporating Social Media into Your Next Event 143

    Event Staging and Promotion 147

    Photos Can Communicate 149

    Online and Blended Events 151

    New Forms of Follow-Up 153

CHAPTER 10. Social Media Stewardship 159

    Deeper, Wider Engagement 160

    Social Bookmarking 162

    Create Raving Fans 165

    Privacy Issues of Social Media Stewardship 167

CHAPTER 11. Media and Public Relations 171

    Your Relationship with the Media Has Changed 171

    Journalists and Social Media 173

    Blogger Relations 175

    Monitoring Social Media 178

    Your Media Release 181

    The Web 2.0 Media Room 184

    Social Media and Crisis Management 188

    When to Take It Offline 190

CHAPTER 12. The Ongoing Cycle of Giving 193

BONUS ONLINE EXTRAS 197

FOREWORD

I F YOU ARE IN THE BUSINESS of raising money for a nonprofit or charitable organization, you may have noticed that the fundraising world has changed with all of the social media opportunities that now exist. Effective fundraisers know how to utilize all of the tools that are available to them; and, therefore, must stay current with the development of all social media opportunities that are coming into the marketplace.

But fundraising success is still dependent on friend-making skills. The key element is learning how to use the myriad of social media opportunities to enhance your ability to become friends with potential donors. That is the essence of Sherrie Madia's book. Dr. Madia walks you through the social media opportunities so that these tools are understandable to you as a fundraiser, and she shows you how to utilize these tools in a manner that will increase your fundraising success by increasing valuable points of donor and prospect engagement.

The purpose of this book is to show fundraisers for nonprofit and charitable organizations how to increase their productivity by connecting more often and more effectively with both current supporters and by targeting potential donors. This book is a comprehensive summary of the concepts, principles, techniques and strategies of fundraising through the use of social media. It demystifies the technological confusion around social media for fundraisers, and identifies the opportunities social media presents to advance the fundraising profession.

Smart, progressive and ambitious fundraisers will be well-served to read, comprehend and implement the strategies outlined by Dr. Madia. In today's fast-paced world, finding quick and fresh ways to make your fundraising case and to advance your donor relationships can make all of the difference in fundraising success. Let Dr. Madia show you the way!

Dave O'Brien
Associate Teaching Professor, Drexel University

ACKNOWLEDGMENTS

I AM GRATEFUL FOR THE DEDICATED group of individuals who helped to make this book possible, including Leann Harms, Jason Karpf, Kristie Lorette, Robert Moskowitz, Jodi Ochstein and Michelle Zehr, among many of my colleagues in the nonprofit field who offered unsolicited stories they thought would be helpful to me and useful for the book, shared their own experiences, and helped to lend credence to the strategies outlined within this book as they implemented them within their own nonprofit organizations.

I would also like to thank my friend Dave O'Brien for writing the foreword. Dave has long served as a mentor to me, from more than a decade ago when he served as Temple University's Director of Athletics, and hired me as Assistant Athletics Director of Development Communications. Our job was to raise funds for a football training complex for the Temple Owls. A few things were against us: (a) Our core constituents wanted a football stadium—not a training facility; (b) we were fighting against the odds of keeping college football alive in the wake of Penn State and the naysayers who said Philadelphia simply couldn't support a Division I college football team, and (c) just after we had launched our fundraising campaign on behalf of the facility, we were dealt a tough blow: Temple had been kicked out of the Big East conference. It seemed as if the sky was falling.

And yet, in this perfect storm for abandoning ship, we didn't lose a single fundraising commitment that had been made. In fact, the football training facility fundraising was an overwhelming success, which I and others attribute to Dave's leadership. When I think about relationship building of any kind, but particularly relationship building toward engagement on behalf of a cause, Dave is the master. In fact, if every fundraising professional engaged his or her constituents like Dave O'Brien—always authentic, always consistent in his messaging from a one-on-one meeting to an arena-sized crowd, and always genuinely interested in forging the long-term relationship instead of the short-term donation, well, perhaps we wouldn't need to rely upon social media nearly as much as we do today. But then, if you are lucky enough to have a Dave O'Brien at your organization, social media can only help to bring the message to more people faster and more efficiently.

INTRODUCTION

W HEN I SET FORTH TO WRITE *The Social Media Survival Guide* series several years ago, I knew I needed to write about social media and business, and social media and job search. With the success of *The Social Media Survival Guide: How to Grow Your Business Exponentially with Social Media*, I experienced many opportunities to talk to—and with—people from across industries and organizations—from solopreneurs to global corporations, to government officials and others in between. The one takeaway from these experiences is this: We can make no assumptions when it comes to social media.

I am often asked, "What is the *best* platform I should be using to promote my business?" or "Can you give me a quick plan so I can go and 'do' social media?" While well-intentioned, these are simply the wrong questions to ask. Rather, the questions any organization must start with are the basics of knowing your objective, your audience, and your resources, and then shaping a strategy and tactics designed to support this.

Having devoted the majority of my career to the nonprofit sector, more than two decades of experience in shaping relevant communications have given rise to this book. In so many respects, social media solves for the age-old questions we have been trying to solve in the nonprofit sector: How to get target groups engaged or reengaged. How to generate an event, a message, an element of engagement that will elicit opt-in participation. And more importantly, how to activate target groups—members, volunteers, alumni, board members, corporate sponsors, clubs, associations, donors—in a manner that generates organic, peer-to-peer conversation to give under-resourced nonprofits an expanded ground force on behalf of their causes.

Social media answers all of these questions for organizations who take a strategic and thoughtful approach to what these online platforms can do, keeping in mind that everything we do in the online space is about an offline effect—that is, real-world actions in the form of volunteerism or making a donation. Nonprofit organizations have not generally held the reputation of being first-adopters of the latest trends in communications technologies—not for lack of creativity, innovation and ingenuity, which are, in fact, the hallmarks that characterize the spirit of the nonprofit workforce, but because they are often in the position of needing to focus on the day-to-day, operational side of maintaining, sustaining, and enhancing existing efforts to drive the organization's mission.

Social media brings to the charitable organization a new raison d'être in terms of adoption. Social media, which simply defined is a new set of engagement strategies, enables organizations to work from a level playing field. While organizations think that social media means *more* work, what it really means is *different* and often more effective work, in that it is based on the principles of time-shifted, 24/7, as-they-like-it content, with a dose of user-generated activity to sustain the need for ongoing dialogue. It is the most viable and attractive answer to one of the longest-standing needs of the nonprofit: human resources.

Who Should Read This Book?

Thus, *The Social Media Survival Guide for Nonprofits and Charitable Organizations* is a "must read" for anyone attempting to fundraise on behalf of a nonprofit organization. Social media tactics enable fundraisers to not only target their donor base more effectively, but also target additional donor pools that they may not have considered in a pre-Web 2.0 (interactive media) environment. The pages that follow cover strategic uses of social media designed so that you can effectively utilize social media techniques to engage, cultivate, solicit and steward your causes. Throughout the book, you'll find case studies of charitable organizations that have employed social media techniques to advance their work. Tapping into social networks enables those responsible for growing constituents and raising funds to optimize their efforts by adding new forms of value—in knowledge dissemination, engagement, access, accountability and more, and delivering this value to supporters and potential supporters in a manner that is flexible and extensible as the organization evolves.

If you are charged with overseeing anything from an alumni affairs office to an annual fund, planned giving, major gifts, a capital campaign, or other fundraising areas—whether you are a small not-for-profit or a large organization, *The Social Media Survival Guide for Nonprofits and Charitable Organizations* will arm you with the tools you need to raise funds successfully by creating additional—and essential—touch points of engagement and bringing the lifecycle of the donor full circle in real and tangible ways using the online space.

CHAPTER 1

The Online State of Nonprofits and Charitable Organizations

E VERYWHERE WE TURN THESE DAYS, regardless of industry, education, or actual usage, people are talking about social media, social networking and social marketing. This results in organizational reactions as diverse as chalking it up to hype and a passing fad, to organizations running at social media platforms at breakneck speed. Somewhere between these two extremes is where your charitable organization should be. Even several years back, it was okay for nonprofits to maintain a healthy skepticism about social media—after all, with limited resources, organizations must be smart with how they spend their financial and human resources. But in the brief span of recent history that marks the era of social media, we have amassed sufficient data to tell us that certain elements of social media—beginning with the premise of deeper and more authentic engagement between consumer and brand, client and provider, constituent and cause—are here to stay.

Information consumers have found that being given a voice and the ability to contribute to the story of a brand or a cause simply feels good. It is emotionally and psychologically satisfying to tell our stories, share our comments, offer our insights—and actually be heard and responded to. We won't give up this newfound power any time soon.

And organizations have found that enabling consumers and clients and constituents to help tell their story also makes sense. Across the board, organizations have determined that the rewards of authentic, organic engagement in a more intimate and targeted way far outweigh the risks, which can include negative comments, opinions and concerns organizations hadn't planned for, such as issues tangential to core interests.

SNAPSHOT: WORLD WILDLIFE FUND

For more than 45 years the World Wildlife Fund (WWF) has been working toward a mission to conserve nature and its inhabitants. With approximately 1.2 million members in the United States and nearly 5 million internationally, WWF uses social media to connect with their global supporters, educate members about conservation issues and keep everyone informed of the latest conservation news.

In addition to conventional social media platforms, including Facebook, Twitter, LinkedIn and a YouTube channel, WWF also maintains member communities on other social networks such as Care2 and Change.org. While these alternative networks are open to anyone who wants to create a profile and join, they provide smaller online communities where WWF members and supporters can connect with one another and post messages and discussions that are relevant to WWF causes.

Panda Pages present a unique and ongoing WWF fundraising initiative that allows members to create their own individual Panda fundraising pages by first choosing a template for their page and then adding photos. Members set their own fundraising goal and can then share links to their fundraising page through email, as well as Facebook and Twitter.

In July 2009, WWF launched another social media initiative to encourage members to put pressure on world leaders attending the G8 Summit in Italy to put more focus on environmental concerns. The campaign incorporated a game, Face the G8, which was created in conjunction with the creative firm Playgroup, and Flickr, where members could post campaign posters and visual petitions. The game required players to act as members of the G8 and make decisions on climate change. Players learned how well they performed as leaders through a personalized video at the end of the game. With more than 10,000 actions taken in the first week, Owen Gibbons, campaign lead for the project revealed, "Our primary objective was to get people to take action as part of our Global Deal initiative. We also wanted to raise awareness of why climate change as an issue should be important to the G8."[1]

[1] Nicola Smith, "Vertical Focus: Charities. Case Study: WWF uses social media to target G8 Summit," *New Media Age*, September 24, 2009, 23.

As a result of the hype, the rapid iterations of social networking platforms, and the real value these platforms provide, the social media space naturally presents a tempting new realm for nonprofit organizations to explore in terms of targeting supporters, generating funds and creating overall impact.

In discussing the transformative power of social media for nonprofits, Dave Kerpen, CEO of the social media leveraging firm Likeable Media, notes, "Not only can tools like Facebook and Twitter help raise funds and awareness for organizations, they can strengthen relationships between supporters and the cause, as well as among stakeholders."

Recent experience provides ample evidence that people responsible for nonprofit leadership—including such fundraising efforts as annual or planned giving, major gifts and capital campaigns—can benefit greatly from the additional points of engagement and the tools for nurturing the full life cycle of each donor that social media can provide.

The terms "charitable organization," "nonprofit," or "not-for-profit" refer to those organizations holding 501(c)(3) status. To be recognized as a nonprofit, tax-exempt charity under section 501(c)(3) of the Internal Revenue Code, an organization must be set up and operated exclusively for exempt purposes set forth in that section, and none of its earnings may advantageously affect any private shareholder or individual. In addition, it may not direct any substantial part of its activities toward influencing legislation, nor may it participate in any political campaign activity for or against candidates.

Although the requirements are stringent, the sector is quite large. According to Beth Kanter, CEO of Zoetica, which provides nonprofits and socially conscious companies with online marketing services, there are approximately 1.5 million nonprofit organizations in the U.S., employing about 13 million people and accepting more than $300 billion in annual revenues.

A Pervasive Medium

Still relatively new, social media has already been put to work by the vast majority of U.S. nonprofits, including Catholic Charities USA, The Salvation Army, American Red Cross, Habitat for Humanity International and Easter Seals. In fact, the first longitudinal study of social media usage by the largest U.S. charities compared 2007 and 2008 social media activity among the top 200 such institutions. The research, conducted by Barnes and Mattson in association with the

University of Massachusetts at Dartmouth[1], shows that nearly 90% of charitable organizations are currently using some form of social media, such as blogs, podcasts, message boards, social networking, video blogging and wikis.

According to the report, social networking in general and video blogging in particular are now in use by nearly 80% of charities. Three-quarters of the responding nonprofits said they monitor the Internet for mention of their name and activities. About 90% of these nonprofits felt their social media activities were successful, and more than 80% said that continued use of social media will be important in the future, with more than 45% singling out fundraising as an important direction for their social media efforts.

Social Media in Action

Examples of social media successes for nonprofits abound. Carie Lewis, director of emerging media at The Humane Society of the United States, reports that her organization uses social media technology to message its supporters individually, and that the goal is to respond to the majority of messages received using these same channels. While this takes a good deal of staff time, leaders at The Humane Society believe it is this "individual engagement" that has made the organization successful in today's technological environment.

---

[1] "Nonprofit Organizations Lead the Way in Social Media Adoption: According to Society for New Communications Research Chair Dr. Nora Ganim Barnes and Eric Mattson of Financial Insite," *Society for New Communication Research*, June 29, 2009, http://sncr.org/2009/06/28/ nonprofit-organizations-lead-the-way-in-social-media-adoption-according-to-society-for-new-communications-research-chair-dr-nora-ganim-barnes-and-eric-mattson-of-financial-insite/

Enchanted Makeovers, which helps provide more comfortable shelters for homeless women and children, has successfully used Martha Stewart's Dreamers Into Doers social networking site to connect with women, assemble a staff, contact crafters and artists in many different countries to lend a hand, and build its own brand. Social media has also proven useful when mentoring others to replicate the group's activities in such distant locations as Singapore and Australia.

The San Francisco Symphony has built its own social network, and is working to integrate social media into more of its marketing efforts. The Symphony recently organized an online contest offering tickets to its opening gala. Dozens of Symphony supporters evidenced their engagement by providing original stories and videos showcasing their personal interests in the Symphony's musical offerings.

The Angela Shelton Foundation has successfully used social media to galvanize hundreds of supporters into action, as well as to make connections with other nonprofits across the country that are similarly working to combat sexual abuse, and to stimulate deeper levels of cooperation amongst groups.

According to an article written by Sumac Research and published on CharityVillage.com:

Epic Change organized the first Twitter-based fundraiser—dubbed "Tweetsgiving"—and raised more than $11,000 in the 48 hours before Thanksgiving 2008 to help build a classroom in Tanzania. In 2009, they repeated the strategy and raised $35,000 in the same two-day period. The nonprofit called charity: water raised more than $250,000 from 10,000 new donors with an online event that brought together Twitter communities from all over the world in February 2009, and separately raised more than $100,000 via its Facebook cause page.

Within hours of the January 12, 2010 earthquake in Haiti, the American Red Cross established a mobile giving program that encouraged people to text the word "Haiti," triggering a tsunami of $10 donations that quickly totaled $32 million. Greenpeace urged supporters to become involved by creating personal fundraising pages in support of its Great Whale Trail campaign, and raised more than $120,000. Crohn's and Colitis Foundation of Canada held its annual gala online and raised an average of $11,130 per committee member—in total, more than $375,000.

Lupus Foundation of America uses a Facebook cause page to engage members by sharing news and asking for help. In six months, membership increased by 584% and online donations via Facebook ballooned by 790%. MomsRising developed an online video campaign that caused membership to explode from 140,000 supporters to 1.1 million.

Social media initiatives generally aren't dry, either. Nonprofit Technology Network (NTEN) accumulated $10,000 in scholarship money for people to attend its annual conference by letting online donors choose which of three embarrassing stunts Executive Director Holly Ross would do if NTEN raised the full amount. Holly wound up remaking Beyonce's "Single Ladies" video, which played on two 30-foot TV screens during the opening session of the group's 2009 Nonprofit Technology Conference.

The list goes on and on. In fact, a recent survey conducted by CharityVillage found more than 80% of the responding nonprofits are currently using social media to accomplish specific goals, among them, to:

- Promote the organization—83%
- Attract new members—56%
- Increase event registration—44%

- Receive donations—33%
- Attract support from younger people—28%

Other reported uses for social media by nonprofits include communicating with volunteers and staff, facilitating public awareness and education, finding new fundraisers, general networking, promoting a cause, prospecting for donors, researching and exchanging information with other nonprofits.

What Your Nonprofit Can Do With Social Media

While social media is varied and flexible enough to support a wide range of activities, at present the most popular and promising uses among nonprofit organizations include the following:

Donations

A growing use of social media is to facilitate donations. According to Sumac Research and Sea Change Strategies, the high net worth, one-percent of donors who are responsible for 32% of all nonprofits' annual gifts actually prefer giving online. To facilitate this, each nonprofit should make it easy for website visitors to learn about its mission, goals, objectives and work, as well as its disbursement of donations and contributions. The site should also have a "Donate Now" button on every page that brings donors straight to a form that allows quick and easy gifting, preferably with an option to use a credit card or other online giving mechanism such as PayPal.

Internal and External Communications

Social media is not a one-way communication: it is focused on the idea of the conversation, and as such, is well-suited as a vehicle for sharing information and receiving feedback among the various stakeholders associated with a nonprofit. Messages to board members, staff, volunteers and others can be personalized through social media, which can be set up to facilitate both individual responses and more widespread sharing based on organizational and social media policies.

Social media also offers opportunities to simply listen. By helping stakeholders communicate with each other, as well as provide feedback, your organization can develop a detailed map of the interests and preferences of people who connect with you, as well as record any positive and negative impressions they may have formed. This is powerful, qualitative data to analyze and incorporate as you fine-tune messages, develop new, programmatic initiatives, reach out to new audiences and attract more support.

In addition, social media permits key members of a nonprofit to develop and build the various sets of messages to be communicated to the public, and to coordinate the dissemination of these messages by making sure every potential spokesperson is on the same page— this becomes a vital communications consideration in the wake of media-savvy constituencies and donor communities.

One Caveat

Social media is also fundamental for building an online community, which can greatly increase the online footprint and thus, the visibility and credibility of any nonprofit. One caveat is that while building online communities is often enjoyable, it's a mistake to become so enraptured with this work that the organization neglects its traditional offline communities—particularly volunteers, donors and other supporters. While it may seem that most people are online these days, tens of millions are not—that's important to remember. Allowing the organization's online presence to intimidate or alienate those who prefer to stay offline can lead to unwanted pushback and detrimental outcomes. In addition, no charitable organization can afford to neglect its primary website. Unlike social media platforms, the organizational website is a space that the nonprofit has under its complete control, so strive to keep it updated and well trafficked.

Use Social Media Technology in New Ways to Do New Things

The uses and technological advances of social media are expanding rapidly, and are limited only by the imaginations of nonprofit leadership. Here are some of the more popular implementations:

Blog. The notion of the "blog" (derived from the words "web log") is the starting point for a great deal of social media activity. Whether the organization designates a single person to control its social media outreach or whether several people are authorized to represent the organization via social media, every project, meeting, decision, program, event, milestone and activity can be mentioned in a blog that is disseminated, automatically or manually, throughout your organization's social network (that is, through your network of social media platforms). Your blog posts don't have to be long. In fact, the average post is between 250 and 500 words.

Importantly, blogs are centered on shareability. That is, every blog should include a Real Simple Syndication or RSS feed that enables readers to subscribe and have the blog content delivered straight to them in the form of an email, a link and more.

While it may be tempting to turn the "Comments" feature off, this will turn your blog into an instant piece of static-ware, as opposed to the rich conversation it was meant to be. If you are looking to use a blog as a touch point for commentary, insights, reaction and dialogue, keep the Comments feature turned on, and monitor the comments regularly. Of course, if you must monitor comments first for any number of reasons, you can set your defaults so that you'll have that option. But be sure to stay on top of the comment review to keep input flowing to your site, or you'll defeat the purpose of timely interaction.

One more point to keep in mind is that links are the currency of the blogosphere, so you'll want to include hyperlinks to other sites you have mentioned within your post so that your blog post grows more "legs" and reaches more people in the online space.

Build and maintain the passion. It's easy, amidst all this technology, to lose track of what drives your organization's success. Most likely, it's a goal and an effort that stimulate some degree of passion in the hearts and minds of your constituents, motivating them to support you. That interest and passion are central, and should never become lost in the whirl and excitement of your organization's social media activity. It takes perspective and focus to keep social media efforts subordinate to and supportive of the organization's mission statement and programs.

Create more popular offline and online events. One of the ways that social media functions effectively is to develop an audience and to keep this group apprised of the latest doings they're likely to care about. Organizations that work the social media space effectively can leverage this capability to attract more participation in their regular events. They can also utilize Internet technology to create new events—webinars, online meetings, interactive activities, and so forth—events that wouldn't otherwise be practical from a budgetary or logistical standpoint.

Get to know your audience better. One of the most powerful promises of social media is the potential to know your constituents and stakeholders in more depth and detail. Familiarity with social media technology allows you to combine what you already know about people associated with your organization (e.g., names, email addresses, physical addresses) with a great deal of additional information they readily provide about themselves through their online activities. You can use various social media analysis tools to find out more (in the aggregate) about their interests, their activities, what media they consume, how they spend their time, even where they shop and what they buy. Various tracking tools and social media measurement tools allow you to research how people are finding and using your online information. As you unlock these details, you can begin to optimize your online presence to increase your audience and your revenues.

Invite participation. In the old days, organizations invited potential supporters to make contact by posting their telephone number in core communications. That still works. But now, this is augmented by technologies that allow people to make their first contact with your organization by texting a message or posting on a web page. For example, a simple invitation on your website, your outbound emails, your car, your t-shirt, or your exhibition booth—something like "Text to *1234567* with your name to be entered in a drawing to win *XYZ*"—makes an extremely attractive and powerful outreach tool.

Make tools and resources available. Social media helps to more widely disseminate information about your organization, so it makes sense to augment your social media efforts by providing online tools and resources—including donation forms, brochures, flyers, posters, box office or ticket-purchase systems and more— right where people in your social network can easily find them. It takes a little time, money and technological know-how to create these online resources, or to digitize their offline counterparts, but they facilitate greater involvement. Because social media supports the rapid distribution of graphics, audio and video, certain platforms can also help to ensure that every potential spokesperson in your organization stays on message.

Post photos and videos online. People enjoy looking at visual material, and they tend to enjoy it even more when they see themselves and people they know. Today it's cheap and easy to take thousands of photos and shoot hours of video at every gathering, and then post the best bits online. "Tagging" people in these photos and videos alerts your social network to the presence of these materials, and generally draws a more engaged online crowd. Social media tools then make it easy for people who see these materials to share them with others they know. Pretty soon, your photo or video has "gone viral" in the sense that your message is reaching people who otherwise might never learn about your organization.

One item to note: You may wish to provide a note indicating how photos and video might be used within your social networks so that participants are aware ahead of time, and any individuals wishing to be excluded can opt out. In essence, this functions somewhat like a media release, which ensures against potential backlash from individuals who may be featured. Remember, the goal is to create community, not unhappy people.

Post your location(s) online. New technology now allows those who feel comfortable with social media to share and respond to details of their whereabouts and about specific venues nearby. The next time you hold an event, for example, you can use location-based technology, such as foursquare, to let people know where you are and what you are doing. People who monitor this type of content (which syncs up with all of the major social networks, including Facebook and Twitter) will be able to drop by and participate. You can also create a location-based online presence for your organization, essentially posting the organization's name, address and contact information in an online database that makes your organization available based on location. By attaching a "nonprofit" tag, you'll attract people who are looking to support charities at your specific location(s) or within your service area(s). These same databases enable people to document their attendance at your events, and in the foursqaure application, enabling the person with the most check-ins to become the "Mayor" of your organization's foursquare application. Talk about creating brand ambassadors! Plus, this has the effect of immediately advising everyone in a user's personal social networks about your organization and its activities.

Recycle media mentions. Creating online "alerts" that deliver your links to media mentions of your organization and its stakeholders can provide a fair amount of substantive fodder for social media outreach. It's easy to recycle these news stories, blog items, links to your web pages, and other online references by sharing them through your social networks. This not only helps keep your organization "top of mind" for people who matter, it provides a pat on the back for those who are working hard to help you meet the organization's goals.

Tell your story. Many organizations use social media to replicate their offline fundraising activities. They ask for support in the same old ways, simply migrating to blogs and tweets, in place of direct mailings and telephone solicitations. This can be a big mistake. Social media represents a new communications paradigm, which requires a new messaging construct. With virtually unlimited online pages, you call tell your stakeholders a great deal about what's going on inside the organization, as well as who's working on various programs and projects, the progress to date and next steps.

The more you reveal through social media about the personalities and activities within the organization, the more points of interest you are providing to which your constituents can respond. If yours is like most nonprofits, there's a clear seasonal pattern to your activities and your fundraising results. Naturally, you'll want to use social media to magnify your impact on donors when and where it counts most. But you can also use social media during your off-season(s) to build a larger, stronger community and position your organization to reap bigger rewards when you once again turn up the heat on your fundraising efforts at points such as the close of a fiscal or calendar year.

Attract younger people, but include all age groups. Have you noticed that younger people are naturally drawn to today's most advanced technologies? While the age demographic continues to skew upward, still, nonprofit organizations can take advantage of the affinity for social media of younger generations by utilizing technology to support more of their decision-making, activities and overall presence. The inevitable result will be more opportunities for young people to get involved, have an impact, and accept leadership roles within the organization. That said, organizations would be remiss in taking an approach that involves the wholesale scrapping of attracting people over the age of 30—or 45 or 60 through social media channels. There are undeniable and important advantages to be gained for organizations that use social media to more fully mine the ideas, energies, and talents of all demographics.

According to Alia McKee, Principal, Sea Change Direct Marketing, "Social networks are a great place to engage in multi-way conversations with a nonprofit's online community and build brand awareness. These conversations cultivate potential donors and reach new prospects. However, with that said, few organizations have made social networks work for large-scale fundraising."

McKee's primary recommendation is that nonprofits "… think multi-channel. Their website needs to be top-notch. Their donation forms need to be tested and optimized. Their email communications need to be engaging and relevant. Their social media presence needs to be authentic and personal. Their online and offline messaging need to integrate. Their PR team needs to drive traffic. When all of these channels are syncing up, that's when online fundraising is at its most successful."

Says Likeable Media's Dave Kerpen: "The beauty of social media for nonprofits is that it truly levels the playing field. Even a nonprofit without huge existing funding channels can use social media to tap into its core constituency, ignite a movement, and better serve its mission."

Indeed, the power of social media for the charitable institution is its ability to serve as the great neutralizer. When used properly, social media can create equal opportunity, giving the newly minted nonprofit the same opportunities as the larger, well-established charities.

CHAPTER 2

Your Organization and the
New Media Landscape

Social Media for Nonprofits: Risk vs. Reward

THE CONSTANT AND CONTINUED GROWTH of social media provides a new opportunity for nonprofit and charitable organizations to prosper. In the past, these organizations have had the tendency to work with familiar one-way marketing tactics. These one-way, "push" messages include direct mail, print newsletters, fundraising events, email and the telephone. With the growth of social media came the need for two-way or "push-pull" communication. Two-way communication provides nonprofit and charitable organizations the opportunity to build community, generate collective action, increase productivity, and grow social and cultural capital and capacity.

According to the Center for Marketing Research at the University of Massachusetts, Dartmouth, use of social media by nonprofits has outpaced the nation's largest corporations and academic institutions. Nonprofit organizations are demonstrating acute awareness of the importance of Web 2.0 and moving forward with it tactically. However, as with any business venture, implementing social media in the nonprofit industry comes with both risks and rewards.

The Risks

From security to posting, nonprofit organizations must be aware of the risks of engaging in social media before they launch a social media campaign. Knowing the risks can help to reduce in advance any unwanted effects or potential negative consequences. The social media mandate for any organization is to maximize opportunity, while minimizing risk.

Security. According to a 2010 study by Lawyers.com[1], 44% of those surveyed reported concern that the personal information they share on social media sites is being used against them. Nearly half of American social media users believe they do share too much information online. Weak privacy settings can lead to dangerous use of personal information. Individuals release personal plans, travel information, contact information, and use credit cards on social media sites to make purchases or donations. While a majority of social media users ignore the risks, nonprofits need to take into account what might happen when Americans wake up and take action to avoid potentially serious consequences from online breaches. Will users continue to make donations via social media? Will they be comfortable with posting contact information online? The questions will continue as platforms and usage evolve,

---

[1] Alison Diana, "Americans Ignoring Social Media Privacy Risk," *Information Week*, October 25, 2010, http://www.informationweek.com/news/security/privacy/showArticle.jhtml?articleID=22 7900690&cid=RSSfeed_IWK_All

but knowing this potential uncertainty demonstrates why multiple channels for messaging are always a smart move.

It is not just social media users who need to be aware of the potential disaster that can strike by logging on and using personal information on social media sites. The nonprofit organization is opening itself up to potential security hazards. Employees who find themselves on social media sites for both business and personal reasons could very well be exposing their companies to a variety of risks. According to the 2010 study *Social Media: Business Benefits with Security, Governance, and Assurance Perspectives*, malware, brand hijacking, lack of content control, noncompliance with the rules of recordkeeping, and unrealistic expectations of Internet security performance are among the risks of social media used for business. A simple lack of awareness on the part of the nonprofit employee can open the door to a wide variety of unwanted threats.

Postings. Within the 2010 study cited above, ignoring golden-rule issues such as common courtesy can cause disgruntled customers. John Cass at Pace Communications indicates that common courtesy can be as simple as asking customers or partners for their permission before blogging about them. In addition, a nonprofit should also pay attention to copyright and fair-use agreements. Nonprofits must also follow basic blogging rules, including clearly stating when a post has been changed, updated, or revised. Posting comments, blogs, photos and videos without the appropriate permission can lead to a host of unwanted headaches in the social media industry.

Nonprofits will also want to protect themselves against liability risks by securing trade secrets and proprietary intellectual property. According to Phil Eschels of Greenebaum, Doll, and McDonald, a firm focusing on labor and employment laws, even somewhat proprietary information should not be placed on Facebook pages or blogs. If you have any doubts about whether content should be placed in the public domain, consult your legal counsel *before* putting anything out there.

Nonprofits also need to be careful about what their employees say and post on social media sites. Anyone responsible for updating a social media page should never say anything that can be viewed as discriminatory or libelous. A simple social media policy that is in place before any premature posting or commenting can easily cut down on social media risks. The social media policy must spell out the rules of engagement for employees (e.g., Are they able to blog on your organization's topic on their own and if so, will they need to include any disclaimer language? Can they tweet and update status during business hours? If they will be using social media on behalf of your organization, what tone and style must they assume?). The document you provide doesn't have to be long or overly complicated, but it should lay down some ground rules so that employees know what is in scope and what is out of bounds.

Employee Usage. Employees or volunteers of a nonprofit organization can often pose the biggest risk in running a social media campaign. According to the Information Systems Audit and Control Association (ISACA)[2], employees create social media risks in the following ways:

- Personal use at work
- Personal use outside of work
- Business use

---

[2] "Social Media: Business Benefits with Security, Governance, and Assurance Perspectives," 2010, http://www.isaca.org/Knowledge-Center/Research/Documents/Social-Media-Wh-Paper-26-May10-Research.pdf

Employees should never use personal accounts to communicate work information. The disadvantages to this danger are many, including risk of privacy violations and a loss of competitive advantage. A loss of competitive advantage can occur if trade secrets or other proprietary information is purposely or accidentally leaked. This can also be highly damaging to the reputation of the nonprofit organization. A nonprofit organization with a tarnished reputation will struggle to stay afloat—donations will slow or cease, along with volunteer interest. In addition to the social media policy, the organization should have procedures in place to enforce policy compliance, and to train employees and volunteers on the proper way to conduct social media business on behalf of the nonprofit.

Copyright Infringement. Social media can create a number of legal issues. Company-branded pages that may be found on Facebook, Twitter, YouTube and other social media sites can create legal issues around the monitoring and removal of content, trademarks, copyright infringement, privacy policies and publicity rights. An organization must review the terms of service a social media site provides before signing up. That said, the roles of the brand police have certainly shifted with the advent of social media. For example, whereas organizations used to chase down rule-breakers with a cease-and-desist, the Web 2.0 environment calls for a kinder, gentler approach to corporate logo use in which companies seek to provide logos, graphics, tag lines, badges, widgets and other assorted graphics, images and content to facilitate seeding the brand throughout the online space via brand ambassadors.

Solicitation. When a nonprofit utilizes social media for donations with a donation button, this is considered solicitation. Nonprofits are required to register in the states in which they solicit donations.

With social media, people can donate from around the globe, making solicitation a potential problem. In order to avoid solicitation-law problems, nonprofits should only collect donations in the states in which they are registered. Because the rules can vary by state, by organization and by specific tactics, if your organization is uncertain about the rules and regulations of solicitation, consult legal counsel.

Misrepresentation. The legal term *agent* implies that an individual has been authorized to act or make statements on behalf of a nonprofit organization. Without making a distinction, it may be hard to keep separate the nonprofit organization's spokesperson's personal and organizational commenting on social media sites. In order to prevent this issue, a nonprofit should issue a disclaimer on any third-party sites such as Facebook, Twitter and YouTube. The disclaimer can help protect a nonprofit organization against uncontrolled or unrelated content that was not formally authorized.

Protection approaches from risks of social media include:

- Protect the nonprofit organization's logo from being misused or misappropriated. Posting your official logo on your wall for fans to share is fine—in fact, if it is a source of pride for your constituency, the question becomes why *wouldn't* you want them to have this? But include some brief disclaimer language that tells users how your mark or logo can be used, as well as how it cannot. A nonprofit's logo is an official representation of an organization and what it stands for, so you will want to walk the fine line of shareability and control.

- Monitor the content of all social media sites your nonprofit organization is on, daily. By doing so, your nonprofit will be aware of the content posted, along with any buzz, positive or negative. You will be able to react to and solve problems quickly. Most importantly, the organization can proactively engage visitors who are talking about their organization.

- Develop social media policies for the nonprofit organization. For some organizations, building social media use into confidentiality agreements might make sense in terms of preventing abuse of social media. Having only one employee overseeing your social media sites (e.g., monitoring the staff who will create social media, measuring quantitative and qualitative results, and ensuring responsiveness to user-generated comments) will also lessen the risks that might result by having multiple individuals working on separate sites or multiple accounts managed on an individual basis. Appointing one social media coordinator will eliminate both risk and message confusion for your constituents.

- Remove related content on social networks when it simply isn't relevant. Facebook and YouTube post related links and advertisements on the side of their web pages. The social media site may deem these sites as related; however, the nonprofit organization may find these related links and sites in no way germane to the organization. Their association may even be damaging to the image of a nonprofit organization. Sites such as Facebook and YouTube allow users to remove this content. In similar fashion, Facebook allows users to modify which friends are shown on the page, thus making this a great opportunity to "feature" select volunteers, members or donors.

Avoidance Rationale

Social media has rapidly found its place in the operating consciousness of business and nonprofit organizations. Social media allows a nonprofit to quickly and effectively send a message to a large population with very little effort. With its popularity, organizations are virtually forced to get involved or face the potential consequences not only of not being active in the social media world, but becoming invisible or irrelevant to constituents. Further, organizations that feel they are at risk if they enter the social media space are at risk anyway for three main reasons: 1. people are talking about them; 2. people are not talking about them; 3. an organization's competitors are talking to your supporters or potential pipeline of supporters. In sum, sitting on the sidelines is no longer an option.

Why nonprofits avoid social media:

- Perceived lack of time
- Real lack of understanding and awareness
- Management or leadership does not understand the necessity

With nonprofits accounting for the largest amount of social media usage, surpassing even Fortune 500 companies, there are significant risks in avoiding social media campaigns. With a vast majority of companies from a wide variety of industries using the words "follow us on Twitter" or "become a fan on Facebook," it is easy to see why a nonprofit organization may be missing out—organizationally and economically—should it choose to forego the trend.

Unlike other new media, fair or otherwise, social media is a direct reflection on an organization's relevance. Those who are not offering a digitized presence of themselves will simply not be able to compete when it comes to philanthropic dollars and volunteer support. Don't believe it? How many "World Wide Web" holdouts do you see today who are still thriving? While a lack of social media presence does not mean that constituents will simply stop talking about your organization, it does signify missed opportunities to engage and grow supporters and to showcase authenticity and accountability, which more and more donors and volunteers are making a prerequisite of initial and ongoing support.

The University of Massachusetts, Dartmouth study also indicated that 89% of charitable organizations are using at least one form of social media. One of the major risks of not using social media is not complying with the industry norm. Since 2005, many older, venerable organizations—including the American Red Cross, the Humane Society of the United States, the American Cancer Society, Planned Parenthood Federation and the National Wildlife Federation—have all opened their doors to the world wider than ever before through the use of social media (Kanter, 2010)[3]. Study after study, case after case provides proof that effectively run social media campaigns can positively and dramatically impact the objectives of a nonprofit organization.

For example, Livestrong[4] does a standout job of engaging users within its Facebook page. This organization, founded by athlete and

---

[3] Beth Kanter, Alison Fine, et al., *The Networked Nonprofit: Connecting with Social Media to Drive Change*. San Francisco: Jossey-Bass, 2010.

[4] Social media strategy at Lance Armstrong foundation, January 14, 2010, http://www.slideshare.net/franswaa/social-media-strategy-at-lance-armstrong-foundation

cancer survivor Lance Armstrong, has more than 1,222,228 fans and growing who "like" the cause. The Livestrong wall is updated several times a day and Livestrong reaches out to fans by commenting on the cancer-related status of fans and participants. Livestrong offers a range of value-added content, including information on cancer, celebrity cancer experiences and events and merchandise designed to help support cancer research.

Social media has provided sizeable amounts of donations for countless nonprofit organizations. In addition to donations, many charitable organizations also find themselves with increased volunteer rates, overall increased understanding of their causes and a renewed interest in their causes. Well-managed social media campaigns provide nonprofit organizations with tools, funds, resources and individuals willing to help—all of which might not otherwise have been possible. The goal for nonprofits in effective social media use is to understand that the utility of these online platforms lies in understanding that you must position your messages where your constituents can be found—and all signs point to social media.

Questions a nonprofit should consider before making the decision to embark upon a social media commitment:

- Does your organization understand social media, not only as a team of users, but as strategists and professionals? Decide if the nonprofit is comfortable with the risks of using and not using social media. The nonprofit should consider if it is using social media because it feels like is has to or because it believes that social media will help its cause and spread awareness. This will have a direct effect on your level of success.

- Do potential donors and volunteers use social media? This is a critical factor in deciding on the need for a social media campaign.

- Does the nonprofit have the resources to devote to social media? Social media requires ongoing attention. This is not a set-it-and-forget-it mechanism or a one-and-done campaign. This is an exercise in ongoing, long-term relationship building, which must be understood by an organization before heading down the digital path.

Why Every Organization Must Engage in Social Media

- Social media is not a trend. We have sufficient—and strong—research to indicate that these new two-way channels are here to stay. Some may have greater longevity than others, but the smart organization is planning content based on the broader strategy of engagement, as opposed to a specific network. That is, if Facebook disappears or is replaced by something new (Don't think this can happen? Remember Friendster?), your organization must be sufficiently nimble to enable an easy migration of content and strategy to the latest platform. Keep in mind, too, that social media is not just for college students or tech-savvy individuals; people of all ages, from all backgrounds are engaging in social media to some degree, and this trend will only continue to rise as business and industry continue to add value and benefit to these channels. Social media is a routine part of how many people connect with one another and with organizations around the globe. Avoiding social media will shrink the nonprofit's contacts and chances of increasing donations and volunteerism.

- Limited connections. There are more than 500 million users on Facebook, and ongoing upticks in users from across all demographics of age, ethnicity and areas of interest. Consequently, with the ongoing rise in mobile devices—thus bringing technology to groups that would otherwise be left out of the market based on socioeconomic status—charitable organizations simply must care about broader reach and act on it. When a nonprofit organization avoids social media, it is, in effect, limiting the size of its potential audience. In today's economic climate, this is not a situation that any nonprofit can afford.

- Awareness. People use social media to display all types of emotions and feelings. In the event someone claims to have had a negative experience with a nonprofit, a nonprofit that is not on social media would not be aware of such complaints. A nonprofit that is aware of problems and concerns can actively work to fix these issues and create a more satisfied fan base. From the corporate sector, BP presents the strongest example of why being there matters. Because BP had a mostly non-existent social media presence, the aftermath of the oil spill in 2010 left everyone from angry Gulf residents to tweeters and bloggers to fill in the gaps. This resulted in more negative commentary and no one to provide a corporate response. Part of the importance of social media for any organization is to build a base of support *before* you need it, so that when crisis does strike, you have a ready band of constituents who are ready and willing to speak in your defense.

- The statistics of Internet usage tell a phenomenal story. With millions of people from all walks of life using the Internet, the decision to bypass social media can result in loss of potential for incremental growth at little or no cost. Even if offline efforts seem to be getting the job done, supplementing with a smart social media plan can only drive the numbers up higher. Because so much of social media is essentially free, the return on this investment can be off the charts.

SNAPSHOT: BOB WOODRUFF FOUNDATION

The Bob Woodruff Foundation works to ensure that injured soldiers returning home from war are afforded all the amenities they need to integrate back into their families and lives here at home. ReMIND. org was launched as part of the foundation's public awareness campaign to educate the public about the needs of injured veterans. In May 2009, The Bob Woodruff Foundation leveraged the power of Twitter and social media in a fundraising campaign called Tweet to ReMIND. The campaign was set to take place over Memorial Day weekend but the success led to a permanent fundraising effort.

The original goal of the Tweet to ReMIND campaign was $1.65 million, representative of $1 for every American soldier who had served in Afghanistan and Iraq from 9/11 to the launch of the campaign. The foundation collaborated with public relations firm Porter Novelli and asked Twitter users to register at TweetToReMIND.org and pledge to donate $1 per tweet with a minimum of 5 tweets spreading the message about the campaign. Prior to the start of the campaign, Marian Salzman, chief marketing officer at Porter Novelli explained,

"Through the networking power of Twitter, individual participants can take action by spreading the ReMIND.org message."[1]

Two of Woodruff's teenage children rallied a group of 525 teens called the Tweet Team. Each member pledged $5.25 and then worked to $100 each over the weekend by recruiting 100 of their friends to pledge $1. Lee Woodruff, co-founder of the foundation with her husband Bob (the ABC journalist injured while covering the war in Iraq), revealed that President Obama's social media campaign during the election inspired the foundation's effort, saying, "We thought, 'Why not bring that to fundraising … make it also something younger folks can get their arms around?'"[2]

While the foundation wasn't able to reach the $1.65 million goal, they did raise more than $75,000 in just the holiday weekend and more than $100,000 three days after Memorial Day.[3]

---

[1] Porter Novelli Announces Lead Sponsorship of 'Tweet to ReMIND' Social Media Campaign for U.S. Troops, *Marketing Weekly News*, May 9, 2009, 43

[2] Eleftheria Parpis, "Using Twitter to do good: How a nonprofit is leveraging social media to raise money." Creative ideas That Inspire, *ADWEEK*, May 31, 2009, http://www.adweek.com/aw/content_display/creative/features/e3if6074d641b5e57bf84e4a1bf12bec580?pn=2

[3] Ibid.

The Rewards

Perception, as they say, is reality. Never has this premise been more applicable than in the case of social media, which in essence, provides audiences with an immediate snapshot of an organization's relevance. Social media, in fact, has come to define the very essence of for-profit and charitable organizations. It separates those who are savvy from those who are hanging on to older and perhaps less-effective strategies. This becomes an important consideration for nonprofits because they must present themselves as growing, thriving and evolving.

This is far more than just a superficial exercise: it's a matter of stewardship, accountability and cultivation of new supporters. Social media requires a long-term commitment from the nonprofit, beginning with senior leadership. With this commitment comes setting the right expectations, including an understanding that while it takes just minutes to set up a new platform, garnering followers, fans and engaged supporters can take just as long as more traditional approaches. Yet, time and again, organizations report that the dividends of persevering with these new media far surpass many of the older forms of communication (e.g., institutional messages, quarterly newsletters and direct-mail appeals). In fact, social media provides charitable institutions with a chance to shed those communications channels that simply weren't working in the first place, and to trade up for newer, more effective approaches to generating engagement.

Nonprofit organizations report that social media is a productive tool in the nonprofit's marketing campaign. In fact, the University of Massachusetts, Dartmouth study found that, 90% of nonprofit respondents noted this to be the case. Additionally, 80% of these organizations believe that social media is at least "somewhat important" to their marketing strategies.

The 2010 Ventureneer/Caliber report[5] provides nonprofits with a list of key factors that explain the habits best suited to reaping the rewards of a social media campaign. These best practices include:

- With a dedicated 25 hours per week, tweeting daily, publishing blog content and updating social media profiles, a nonprofit's social media campaign can thrive.

---

[5] "10 Highly Successful Social Media Habits for Nonprofits," Ventureneer/Caliber Reports, 2010, http://www.wildapricot.com/blogs/newsblog/archive/2010/11/02/10-highly-successful-social-media-habits-for-nonprofits.aspx?utm_source=feedburner&utm_medium=feed&utm_campaign=Feed%3A+WildApricot+%28Wild+Apricot+blog+on+non-profit+technology%29

- Become a power user. A majority of nonprofits use social media to boost visibility, drive website traffic and build a community. The most effective nonprofit will use social media to raise money, to raise awareness, to engage in advocacy and to advance its efforts through cause marketing.

- Strong nonprofits rely on social media to enhance marketing campaigns, not to reduce marketing. Social media is about increasing cost-efficiency and creating an effective marketing campaign.

More Rewards

- Nonprofits can easily spread awareness of their cause along with connecting with other nonprofit organizations.

- User-generated comments and postings on sites such as Facebook allow users to share their stories with one another and create a renewed awareness of the issues a nonprofit organization is trying to solve for or alleviate.

- Nonprofits can increase their interaction with their target market. Social media has created an entirely new means of interaction. Users are able to comment, participate in polls, ask questions, play games, view photographs and view video that is directly related to the nonprofit organization. Bringing the benefits, testimonials and impact to life for your organization through this content is a powerful means of driving engagement.

- Social media can increase volunteerism for a nonprofit organization. Nonprofits are able to post volunteer opportunities and provide potential volunteers with information on the type of volunteer work and the specifics of their cause. Social media can reach out to prospective volunteers that come from a variety of age groups and walks of life. Individuals who may never have considered the possibility of volunteering in the past may become interested in volunteering based merely on the way in which the volunteer opportunity is presented. And with the ongoing mainstreaming of mobile devices and text-messaging campaigns, charitable organizations can reach potential constituents more easily and effectively. The one-on-one text message (generally received by the audience on an opt-in basis), is one of the most powerful ways of creating an intimate communication in a mass-mediated way.

- Social media can serve as an educational tool. Social media users can be educated on a particular cause. The amount of nonprofits in existence makes it impossible for audiences to become aware of, let alone support every cause. But a social media presence can provide a nonprofit the opportunity to stand out from the crowd when used properly. Blogging, tweeting, commenting, updating status and providing plenty of links to additional content are designed with the intention of pointing users in the appropriate direction of understanding the goals and objectives of a charitable institution. Education is a must-have tool in generating involvement for a cause.

- Social media can reach an entirely new crowd of donors and supporters. Think about the adults in their 20–30s who are likely to never have donated to a cause based on their own economic uncertainty as well as the thought of having to donate substantial amounts of money. Social media sheds light on the idea that a difference can be made, even if it is just one dollar at a time. Tapping into such demographics as they are beginning to seriously consider their values and their value to society can have a lifetime of impact on your organization. Ultimately, the goal of every nonprofit should be donors for life. Hence, social media becomes a brilliant pairing for the nonprofit, with its foundational value in driving community and fostering personal relationships.

With a nominal to zero-based operating cost (the exception being staff time, design and programming and possible outsourcing of content), social media can expand the success and prevalence of a nonprofit without demanding a portion of what is generally a tight budget to begin with. A nonprofit can manage its own online reputation and image as well as engage in conversation with supporters around the globe. If you have constituents who are internationally based, the savings on mailing costs alone is a value-add. And frequency of contact becomes a non-issue.

Nonprofits as a Social Media Training Ground

When a nonprofit has decided to enter the domain of social media marketing, the best place to begin is by educating its audience so that the audience becomes more socially aware of the cause and what donations can do to make a difference. In some cases, organizations begin to engage audiences via social media by becoming the educators in using the media. That is, understanding that individuals may be hesitant to engage in social media, or are unsure where to begin, your organization can provide an opportunity for engagement by offering a workshop, lecture, SlideShare presentation, or webinar on social media basics. After all, we always remember our first teacher, don't we?

Once basic education has occurred, potential donors and volunteers can be further engaged via these new media. In effect, your organization can become the training ground for newer social media users. These channels can then become your most effective tools, as they capitalize on newfound enthusiasm for exciting new ways to communicate. Social media is first and foremost about building relationships around common interests, so every charitable organization will want to use this to its advantage.

Like a relationship with a friend, if you as an organization will be taking a hiatus from blogging or regular updates on your Facebook page, be sure to notify audiences in advance so that they aren't left wondering where you have gone. Give them something to look forward to when you return—like a state-of-the-state update, or a year-end recap and goals for the upcoming year. This communication becomes key in that social media is based on establishing credibility as a trusted advisor. This means consistency, reliability and authenticity at all times. Doing any less can become a black eye for your organization, so you'll want to be sure to build an editorial calendar into your social media strategy to ensure that you are always out in front when it comes to your content.

While there are plusses and minuses to using social media, a nonprofit must be aware of the increasing prevalence of social media as a two-way communication platform. Should a nonprofit decide on the use or continued use of social media, it must be aware of continuous changes in policies surrounding social media. With careful planning and research, a nonprofit can have the best of both worlds: a successful social media campaign that is able to steer clear of unwanted issues. Here again, a simple social media policy can prevent problems down the road.

CHAPTER 3

Assess Your
Online Presence

Stepping into the Social Media Space: Your Web 2.0 Presence

WHEN YOU DECIDE TO COMMIT your organization to the social media space, you must consider many items in advance of a launch. With proper planning and strategy, social media can propel the success of a nonprofit organization in unimaginable ways.

Contrary to the initial belief that social media was a passing fad, the online space has transformed itself from a teenage trend to a full-scale marketing technique. Social media has evolved beyond trendiness, and while it will continue to morph and develop as usage and value continue to grow, we understand enough about the space to realize we must take it seriously as a core part of any marketing strategy. In its brief span of existence, social media has fostered a network of individuals of all ages and backgrounds around the world allowing them to create, share and discuss content in ways that are highly personal and highly engaged.

Social media has already become a powerful tool for nonprofit organizations, enabling more peer-to-peer interaction on a regular basis. This becomes important, particularly for those organizations who hear time and again from constituents, "You only talk to me when you want my money." Now, nonprofits can engage on a daily basis with core groups of supporters to offer value, insights, information and education—all non-financial communications that make for powerful cultivation tools. Nonprofits can use social media to reach out to millions of individuals, often without ever having to pick up a phone to solicit donations.

Social media is becoming more and more prevalent in the nonprofit sector. As mentioned in Chapter 1, a 2009 study[1] conducted by the University of Massachusetts Dartmouth's Center for Marketing Research found that 90% of the largest U.S. charities are using some form of social media. This was a 17% jump from 2008 and an increase of 64% for 2007. Social media is increasing awareness of causes, enhancing the solicitation of donations, recruiting volunteers and advancing the planning of fundraisers and cause-related events. But stepping into the social media space can provide a challenge for anyone unfamiliar with the territory. However with research, planning and clear expectations of what this space can produce, social media can become a tool that will propel a nonprofit organization to new heights when it comes to awareness and involvement.

---

[1] "U.S. Charities' Adoption of Social Media Outpaces All Other Sectors for the Third Year in a Row," University of Massachusetts Dartmouth Center for Marketing Research, August 3, 2010.

Social Media Fundamentals

Social media is predicated on a high level of user interaction. Users can easily create, use, share, view and comment on a wide variety of content. Social media is based on the notion of a two-way interaction—a conversation, as opposed to a one-way, institutionalized message. Traditional media provides content and messages to its readers, listeners and viewers, whereas social media provides visual, text and audio messages to its users, all designed to encourage a response.

Some of the more popular or well-known social media platforms include Facebook, Twitter, YouTube, MySpace, Flickr, blogging, podcasts, LinkedIn, video chat and mobile phone applications.

Relevant to nonprofits, social media can be used to increase awareness, donations and volunteerism. Nonprofits can use social media to tell the story of their organization and provide information to those interested in the cause in a way that even as far as five years ago was simply unfathomable. So, while there is much angst within philanthropic organizations today, with greater need and fewer dollars to go around, these organizations have much to be excited about with this new set of low- to no-cost strategies for engagement.

What is Web 2.0?

Web 2.0 is the term that is commonly associated with information sharing, user-centered websites. Web 2.0 gives users the opportunity to interact with one another in a virtual community that offers time-shifted, as-you-like-it, choice-based content—and a chance to have a voice. The Web 2.0 platform is about providing users with content starters designed to prompt them to respond, to participate, to be part of the experience and to help tell the story and share the story of your organization.

This space is about providing users with a means of easily and seamlessly generating content on behalf of your cause. While some organizations fear this platform because it signals a loss of control, in fact, the control remains with the organization in the form of providing the right types of content starters to facilitate conversation. Though the conversation may not always be the message you'd like to receive or promote, this, too, becomes part of what can make a charitable institution stronger—being able to address concerns, complaints or issues in a manner that is transparent and real. This alone can move an organization past problems and onto a path toward success.

Key Tips for Using the Web 2.0 Space

- Focus on the particular goal of your nonprofit. Do not generalize or talk around the need. If your goal is volunteer recruitment, make this known. For example, the UN Foundation has a website entitled Nothing But Nets. This site focuses solely on providing malaria nets to children who live in developing parts of the world and has experienced wild success, in part, because it focused on just one issue in a manner that was simple, clear and to the point. Asking audiences to focus on complex, multipart pieces of your story can result in message dilution and lack of response.

- Ask for donations other than monetary donations. Nonprofits frequently experience a lack of donors because they are constantly asking for monetary gifts. The Internet is a great place to ask individuals for donations other than money. Even beyond requests for gifts in kind or gifts of time and talent, social media can provide a new type of ask: the gift of content. Asking individuals to share their stories, photos, experiences, or expertise via a blog, video, or photo-sharing site is one of the most powerful means of cultivation because you are, in essence, asking these supporters to share a part of themselves and thus, to become a part of the organization's story.

• Use social media to gather new connections, beginning with other nonprofits. While it used to be that like causes chose to go it alone, hoping for a glimpse of what the competing organization was up to, today's social media space has prompted a new approach to competing dollars: Join them in conversation. For starters, understanding competitors' platforms and strategies is now just a few keystrokes away. Measuring followers, fans, messaging, offers and types of responses is the new basic math.

Generally speaking, there has always been a sound basis of collegiality within the nonprofit world. But for those organizations that may have taken an alternate course, they soon realized that disparaging or snarky comments about the competitor only put them further behind. Therefore, the smartest approach is one of talking openly with peer institutions to work collaboratively on best practices and a shared knowledge base. Often, nonprofit organizations realize the benefits of pairing causes in which one cause or institution can complement the other. This presents a new level of shared fundraising targeted to corporate and foundation relations with specific grant requirements that some organizations simply could not meet on their own.

- Web 2.0 does not mean that a nonprofit organization has to build its own online community. Nonprofits should ease into the Web 2.0 community by making effective use of the existing Web 2.0 tools. Nonprofits can use common Web 2.0 tools to smoothly move into the Web 2.0 community as well as to get their cause and goals out to a broader audience.

- Transition your resources into Web 2.0 slowly. This transition can pose a big challenge for nonprofit organizations, as they must adapt their skills to a new model of communication. As your efforts move toward blogging, tweeting, podcasting and more, you will likely begin to see a change, not only in the content, itself, but in your staff as well, as they reshape their perception of themselves and of the organization overall. That said, allow for plenty of time to ensure that your staff has achieved a comfort level within this space.

- Nonprofits must stay current with what is happening with Web 2.0 and they must pay close attention to what other nonprofit organizations are doing in this space, as this becomes a tremendous learning opportunity. If you're not sure where to start, begin by following, "friending," and tuning in to nonprofits' channels. You'll want to build your own network of contacts in the process so that you can reach out to someone you know in the nonprofit community for advice and insight.

Sharing Your Organization's Story

Social media allows nonprofits of all types to share their story and present their message in a more concentrated way to a broader audience of potential supporters. But in order to do so effectively, an organization must first shape its core messages with clarity and conciseness and in a manner that is donor-centric, capturing the essence of the organizational need, while conveying that essence in a manner that constituents can relate to.

Core Message Points

Social media can be used to get core messages to the right target groups at the right time for the benefit of the nonprofit organization. Nonprofits can relay any message through the use of social media and can use social media to fundraise, increase awareness, put forth a plea for urgent help and recruit volunteers for their cause. Nonprofits can focus on a wide range of goals for using social media, each designed to capture a particular audience interest or need. Social media can aid with fundraising, volunteers, increased interaction, and education—all in real time. While this may not seem dramatic if you are newer to the field, these platforms are a far cry from the twice-a-year, "spring and fall" fundraising appeals of the past, which tended to elicit the reaction from audiences that we only think of them when we consider our fundraising goals.

Another benefit of social media is that it can enhance the efforts of widely known organizations as well as smaller, lesser-known organizations. Focusing on one particular goal is the best way to achieve your organization's objective using social media. Core messages can be presented one at a time—or separate but related messages that make up your organization's core mission can be relayed through different social networks. Once a nonprofit organization reaches one goal, it can move on and work toward a second, third and even fourth goal. Part of the value of starting small and keeping the focus clear is that you will want to gather what you've learned along the way about how your message was received, the impact it had on volunteerism, fundraising and overall engagement. You can then pour these learnings into your next organizational goal.

Fundraising and Microfunding. Many nonprofit organizations are taking advantage of social media when it comes to raising funds. For example, the 12for12k Challenge, which raises funds for a core of charities most in need, has raised more than $100,000 since December of 2008[2] by reaching out to individuals via social media. The best part about funding through social media is that individuals can donate as little or as much as they want with just a few clicks. Social media users can donate small amounts, which can ultimately make a big difference. In fact, charitable organizations are witnessing this dramatic trend toward small donations in larger quantities. In part, this is based on text-based giving platforms, which can accept only smaller donations—but are immediately accessible channels for instant support. This form of microfunding can add up to significant dollars in support of a goal or cause.

Increased Interaction with Audiences. Social media has created a new avenue for nonprofit organizations to interact with their audiences. Users can interact through sites such as Twitter and Facebook. They are able to play games, make comments, watch

---

[2] "The 12 for 12k Challenge" 2010, About page, http://12for12k.org/about/

videos, ask questions and take polls. Nonprofits can interact with thousands upon thousands of individuals, which is something no other outreach program can accomplish.

Volunteer Recruitment. Social media is an effective means of reaching out to potential volunteers. Just as organizations look to the Internet for job postings, nonprofits are able to post volunteer opportunities. In addition to posting these opportunities, nonprofits are able to provide prospective volunteers with information on the cause and the type of volunteer work. Social media can reach individuals who have intentions of volunteering, young people who may have a service requirement as part of course work, retired individuals who may have time to help, and individuals who may never have considered volunteering.

Education. Social media can educate users on particular causes. With so many nonprofit organizations in existence, it is impossible to know what they all support and stand for. Social media gives nonprofit organizations the tools they need to stand out and get the word out regarding their goals. Blogs, tweets, status updates and links are all meant to point users in the direction of understanding the objectives of the nonprofit organization. Education is often the key to getting users involved.

"You may have cultivated networks of donors, event attendees, volunteers, coalition partners, and so on. Internet-based relationship management and communication tools provide a cost-effective means for managing your offline communities, as well as new opportunities for connecting and optimizing these existing networks," wrote Ted Hart, James Greenfield, and Michael Johnston in their book entitled Nonprofit Internet Strategies: Best Practices for Marketing, Communications, and Fundraising Success.[3]

A nonprofit's social media campaign should include:

- A clear objective. It must be easy for users of social media to understand the choice of social networking platforms as it relates to the nonprofit's desired outcome (e.g., sharing stories with fellow alumni using Facebook, or helping to promote a cause via Twitter. That is, the action item must be clear on each platform that is established, such as "stay informed," "share this," "make a donation" or "sign up to volunteer"). Social media should not just be added for the mere fact of hoping it works. For example, if a nonprofit is seeking to create awareness about its particular cause, its social media sites should contain plenty of information to educate users. Information can come in the form of text, video, audio, quizzes and question-and-answer forums.

- A nonprofit social media campaign should have a strong emotional appeal. Whether the nonprofit is feeding needy children, aiding in disaster relief, or saving the planet, the emotions of the social media users need to be reached. Emotions can be reached with visuals, personal stories, or strong, descriptive text. The emotional appeal needs to make users want to act on behalf of the cause of the nonprofit organization.

---

[3] Hart, T., Greenfield, J., et al., *Nonprofit Internet Strategies: Best Practices for Marketing, Communications, and Fundraising Success.* Canada: John Wiley and Sons, Inc., 2005.

- A nonprofit organization should have a well-thought-out strategy before engaging in the use of social media. Social media usage should be specifically designed to target objectives. Depending on time, nonprofits should choose to focus on the forms of social media that they can most benefit from. Nonprofits should not simply place themselves on every available social media site just because these sites can be set up quickly. Social media sites need to be updated frequently. When time is a factor, a nonprofit should focus on one or two social media sites. This ensures the organization will have time to nurture its chosen sites.

Organizational Commitment

As with any marketing campaign, social media requires commitment from the nonprofit organization. When partaking in a social media campaign, organizations need to be all in. A blank Facebook page is far more detrimental than no Facebook page at all. A Twitter account sending one tweet a month might as well not ever have been created. When a nonprofit decides to go with social media, they must stick with it and give each site the attention it requires.

Just as social media is predicated on user involvement, a nonprofit organization needs to be heavily involved in strategizing each site. "Go big or go home" is essentially the attitude to take when engaging in a social media campaign for nonprofits. A hardly existing social media campaign might as well be a non-existent social media campaign. Awareness cannot be raised if a social media site is not actively used.

Many nonprofit organizations chose to forego the idea of a social media campaign because of:

- Lack of time
- Lack of awareness
- Lack of understanding

SNAPSHOT: VALLEY BIBLE FELLOWSHIP CHURCH

Based in Bakersfield, California and with campuses in Las Vegas, Nevada; Colorado Springs, Colorado; Nashville, Tennessee; Reno, Nevada; Valencia, California and Visalia, California, the Valley Bible Fellowship (VBF) church uses social media as a way to streamline multiple church campuses into one online community, where church members can connect and discuss their faith, VBF events and other issues that are important to them. The church makes use of the MyChurch.org social networking site, which functions similarly to Facebook in that members can create their own profile pages and connect with other members affiliated with their church.

In an article for "The Nonprofit Times," Joe Suh, creator of MyChurch.org, explained the appeal of the site is that it is a social network with a Christian slant, adding, "Churches are making much more of a concerted effort to blend into this (social media) culture. It's wise because their members are using things such as Facebook, and it's a way to truly relate to them."[1]

As of August 2010, the Valley Bible Fellowship page on MyChurch.org boasted more than 1,500 members, nearly double the 800 members tallied in a 2008 article for "The Nonprofit Times," in which J. Doss, moderator for the Valley Bible Fellowship page explained the popularity of the page, saying, "Social media sites are just another, easier way for people to keep up with each other and what's going on with the church. With several campuses, this gives us a way to be a single community and support the same effort."[2]

---

[1] Natalie Ghidotti, "Joining the masses online: churches, religious groups outreaching through social media networks," The Nonprofit Times, June 1, 2008, 21

[2] Ibid.

Most professional organizations agree that having at least one or two social media sites up and running is the way to go for overall effectiveness. Not having social media sites as a nonprofit can prove to be a serious error when promoting and gaining support for an organization. When a nonprofit has decided to launch its social media efforts, the best thing to do is to begin to educate and groom the audience so that they become more aware of the cause and what their donations can do to make a difference. Reaching out to potential donors and volunteers through a means they can easily relate to is much more effective than any other traditional form of marketing. Social media is about building relationships.

Resource Audit

Before hitting "enter" to create an account, a nonprofit should take into consideration the time and effort it takes to operate social media accounts. Does the organization have the time and resources to make this project a success? The organization will need the time to devote as well as at least a core of individuals who are social media savvy.

In order to reap the benefits of using social media, nonprofits must be aware of potential barriers that exist. The biggest barrier that occurs when trying to use social media is lack of knowledge of the media and their implications.

Nonprofits must first educate themselves on the various social media outlets. Important to remember is that being a user of social media is dramatically different from being a strategist of social media. This is an element that is often overlooked.

Time permitting, employees can read up on social media. By doing some basic research into core social networking platforms, nonprofits can learn the best way to promote their cause based on their unique value proposition, objectives, audience needs and resources. One option in starting out is to hire a consultant. Be sure this individual is competent in areas outside of social media and familiar with the nonprofit space.

While social media can seem overwhelming at first, many of the same rules of engagement still apply, and the platforms themselves are easy to learn. Organizations wanting to arm a broader staff with the ability to work within the space might consider bringing in an outside consultant to provide technical expertise and best practices in terms of setting up applications, creating an effective content strategy, measuring social media effects and setting the right expectations within the organization.

While there are an inordinate number of "social media experts" willing to sell organizations fancy software packages for monitoring social media, or consulting based on a shallow knowledge of applications as opposed to a deeper understanding of fundraising and communications, most organizations should forego these offers in favor of some basic training by a reputable firm. In so doing, nonprofits can learn the best way to promote their cause *before* they enter the space. An expert in the social media field can lead an organization to a maximum amount of success.

Another option includes hiring an intern. College students can be savvy when it comes to social media and they can be willing to do the work in order to build their resumes and gain valuable experience. That said, we see perhaps too many social media endeavors being given to the intern or the youngest person on the team, as he or she is perceived to know all about these new marketing media, without question. If you can find an intern who does understand how to communicate professionally within this space, by all means take advantage of this, as the prospect of working with social media is an attractive proposition to most people just entering the workforce; they realize this is a skill that will enhance their resumes, and one they will most definitely need. But for best results, offer a writing test to ensure that the selected candidate is able to write professionally in a tone and style that are suitable for your organization.

Many local colleges and professional development centers now offer social media courses, so this might be a cost-effective option when it comes to training your core team. As social media has become an integral part of day-to-day life, colleges are taking advantage of the fact that many young adults and business professionals are going to need to understand social media, especially when it comes to marketing, public relations and business. In fact, social media courses are now being integrated throughout many programs of study.

Social media creates the opportunity for nonprofits to reach out to their intended audiences for little or no cost. Organizations need to create conversation and user engagement that will entice the potential donor or volunteer. Organizations should never use superfluous content; readers are likely to respond negatively—if at all—to this type of rhetoric, as the social media space calls for an honest and genuine communication style.

Using social media can enable your nonprofit to create distinction in the marketplace. As social media continues to evolve, the benefits of regular social media use continue to grow. Social media, when used properly, can enhance the objectives of a nonprofit organization and forever change society's perception of your organization's work.

The plunging economic status of individuals and corporations has taken a toll on many communities and nonprofit organizations. Mainstream social issues, such as hunger, disease or illiteracy are often issues that are too large for any single organization to solve, especially based on the current economic turmoil (Kanter, 2010)[4]. Embracing social media has given these nonprofit organizations a chance to interact with other nonprofits as well as many individuals they may have never been able to reach in the past. A large population of young people has become more and more passionate about social causes and change when organizations relate these causes through social media channels, which many people have become flat-out addicted to.

Stepping into the social media world may be a big step for a nonprofit organization. However, with careful planning, research, time management and a thoughtfully constructed social media campaign, your organization can reach new heights when it comes to donations, awareness and volunteerism.

---

[4] Beth Kanter, Alison Fine, et al., *The Networked Nonprofit: Connecting with Social Media to Drive Change*. San Francisco: Jossey-Bass, 2010.

CHAPTER 4

A New Kind of
Prospect Research

N A 2009 *MARKETING WEEK* ARTICLE, Morag Cuddeford-Jones pointed out, "The emergence of social media has benefitted traditional research methodology by forcing it to become more engaging and interactive."[1]

For years, research pertaining to fundraising campaigns has revolved around traditional approaches including historical comparisons, psychographic data (including inclination, ability and lifestyle), as well as quantitative methods involving evaluations and surveys, and qualitative methods using interviews and focus groups. As social media continues to revolutionize advertising and marketing research for general business, it is also redefining standard research methods for fundraising campaigns.

Social media allows unprecedented access to a charitable organization's constituencies, offering administrators and frontline fundraisers a new dimension in constituent research. As more

---

[1] Morag Cuddeford-Jones, "Market Research: Social media breathes new life into research," *Marketing Week*, May 7, 2009, 25.

and more people join and engage in social media sites, using relevant tools available through various public social networks, creating private social networking sites, and implementing social media monitoring services will become integral to optimizing any campaign research platform (from cultivation, to annual fund, to initiative-specific goals) and actuating real results.

Locating Your Donor Base

While social networks provide valuable quantitative research methods through various survey and polling applications, tapping into public social networks can also provide a useful alternative to traditional, qualitative research employing ethnographic components. Ethnography uses conversation, in-depth interviewing techniques and observation to learn more about people, as well as their influences and perceptions. Social media allows direct access to conversations and comments from willing participants, enabling a whole new dimension in qualitative research.

Of course, to really take advantage of the qualitative and quantitative research benefits available through social media, nonprofit organizations must be engaged with others involved in the online communities they are hoping to gain insight from. A recent *PR Week* article cites that, "Twitter, LinkedIn and Facebook communities can be effective ways to distribute opinion surveys targeting specific groups—particularly for new business and initial research phase," but Eva Keiser, Senior Vice President at Risdall McKinney Public Relations, is quick to add, "Before you blanket social media sites with surveys, establish yourself within the community."[2]

---

[2] "PR Toolbox: Importance of SEO, utilizing social media research, more," *PR Week (US)*, April 6, 2009, 21.

Any charitable organization at any level of maturation should be actively participating in all of the four major social networking sites: Facebook, Twitter, LinkedIn and YouTube. However, the research team within this organization should also be using these networks to compile information on potential supporters—from volunteers, to stakeholders in government and industry, to board members and donors—to more accurately manage the goals of the organization and to make adjustments as needed.

Your Social Media Pipeline

Facebook pages have become imperative for businesses and organizations, as well as cause-based or charitable organizations. Not only does Facebook facilitate an open forum for communication between brands and consumers, as well as nonprofit organizations and their constituents, but they also help to gather fundamental information that researchers and administrators would otherwise spend hours trying to accumulate. Facebook pages can be created to represent an organization or public figure, allowing individuals to show their support by clicking "like."

This will add the page to the supporter's personal profile and allow that individual to interact and engage with others on the page. An organization's Facebook page also provides incomparable demographic statistics about supporters of the page through the "Insights" tool, which analyzes the demographic data with regard to the age and gender of everyone who supports the page. When compared to average Facebook user statistics, researchers can use the information to determine which gender and age groups their cause or campaign has not yet connected with. The data can be viewed in graph form or exported into an Excel file.

Facebook polls are another fast and easy way to ascertain research data through the social networking site. They can be created through the Facebook polling application and added to personal profiles or public pages. You simply create the question and a set of potential responses and share the poll with constituents on your page. The application handles the rest, tabulating the results instantly. Polls can be used to gauge opinions on organizational priorities, how supporters are feeling about a proposed new program or initiative, or any other opinion-based questions.

SNAPSHOT: GREENPEACE INTERNATIONAL

Based in Amsterdam, the Netherlands, Greenpeace International has prided itself on grassroots campaigns to support their mission to protect the global environment. Greenpeace makes effective use of Twitter, Facebook and a YouTube channel to inform and educate fans, followers and subscribers about environmental issues, as well as industries whose operations are detrimental to the environment. Posts are also used to drive traffic between the various social networking platforms and to the organization's website. Social media has proven particularly useful in generating public support and inciting calls to action when it comes to Greenpeace International's environmental campaigns.

After identifying a company responsible for rainforest deforestation and having questionable methods for obtaining palm oil among Nestlé's supply chain, Greenpeace sprung to action by posting a controversial and graphic video likening the consumption of Nestlé's Kit Kat candy bar to Orangutan fingers. Nestlé responded by having the video removed from YouTube, which caused a social media fury over censorship, and Greenpeace supporters spread their outrage via Facebook, Twitter and emails. Within two months of the social media campaign, Nestlé announced a new policy and a commitment to refrain from using products that stemmed from rainforest destruction.

Greenpeace International announced the success of their campaign in a feature article on their website, identifying Facebook as a "key online arena for the Kit Kat campaign where a steady stream of pressure was applied to Nestlé via comments you left on its fan page."[1] The article also thanked supporters who changed their Facebook profile pictures to avatars that showed their support for the Greenpeace International campaign.

---

[1] "Sweet Success for Kit Kat Campaign: You asked, Nestlé has answered," *Greenpeace International*, May 17, 2010, http://www.greenpeace.org/international/en/news/features/Sweet-success-for-Kit-Kat-campaign/

Social Media Tools:
Facebook, Twitter, LinkedIn and YouTube

Going through Facebook's ad creation program will also give you instant access to core demographic information. You don't actually have to pay for an ad to benefit from Facebook's rich, statistical data. Simply go to "Create An Ad" and enter anything in the URL box or, if you have a Facebook Page, click on the option pertaining to advertising something on Facebook. This will take you to the next step where you can choose specific demographic information, narrowing the results down by gender, age, education, geographic information and interests. A floating box will appear in the right-hand column with the total number of people who match your required demographic parameters.

The beauty of Facebook ads is that unlike an expensive ad campaign that you may know isn't working after the initial launch, Facebook ads enable you to monitor in real time, fine-tune elements by modifying content and bid amounts that you are willing to spend per impression or per click-through and turn ads off that you know are not working.

The microblogging site Twitter has introduced another new frontier in social media research. Applications are being developed constantly to improve methods for searching for and locating information on Twitter. Twitter's search engine alone allows a real-time account of what is being said about any keyword that you enter. For the most direct route to discovery for such information as new prospects who might be interested in your cause, visit www. Search.Twitter.com.

Twitter can prove useful in collecting information on like causes, as well as the individuals and corporations supporting those causes. Locating peer or competitor organization's followers on Twitter will enable you to gather data from their profiles and also keep abreast of what they might be saying about you. This can be helpful in pinpointing confusion that some may have regarding an organization's views and goals.

Similar to Facebook, several applications that enable Twitter users to survey their followers have been developed. The most popular of these is Twtpoll at http://twtpoll.com. This site allows Twitter users to create basic polls at no cost. There is a charge for creating more complex surveys, as well as collecting demographic information from participants, but the time saved is well worth the expense. Using social media as a means to conduct surveys and polls is quickly replacing conventional methods that once were limited to mail-in responses and telephone surveys.

With Twitter posts limited to 140 characters, it is primarily used by organizations to provide short segments of information or answers to questions, or as a method for driving traffic back to an organization's website where constituents will find more comprehensive content and other information about the organization or cause. Studying click-through rates using Google Analytics and comparing them to an organization's total number of followers may help determine the fundraising potential behind Twitter. According to a report from Nationaljournal.com, "While no official statistics are available, early data suggest the click-through rate (on Twitter) is in the mid-single digits, delivering much better results than email and other kinds of online advertising."[3]

The professional social networking site LinkedIn also offers tools that could be beneficial to nonprofit researchers. The LinkedIn Answers feature can be used to post questions within different targeted professional groups. For instance, on September 17, 2007, prior to the November 2008 presidential election, then Senator Barack Obama posted this question in the Small Business category: "How can the next president help small business and entrepreneurs thrive?"[4]

He received more than 1,400 unique responses from the small business community. This type of research provides unparalleled advantages in formulating campaign efforts that target the needs of specific professional communities, as well as discovering potential financial contributors.

YouTube can be used to deliver messages to supporters by featuring content such as annual fund ads, testimonials from constituents who have benefitted directly from the organization, interviews with senior leadership and more. Viewer comments can provide a wealth of additional, qualitative data, providing researchers with a dynamic gauge of how the organization is

---

[3] David Herbert, "Will Twitter Add a New Wrinkle to Campaign Fundraising?" *Nationaljournal.com*, April 7, 2009.

[4] LinkedIn Answers, http://www.linkedin.com/answers/startups-small-businesses/small-business/STR_SMB/95900-11932467

perceived. The instant feedback also enables organizations to react quickly to any misperceptions or negative comments a video may have produced.

There are also public social networks geared toward specific ethnic groups. MiGente is the largest social network specifically aimed at Latino-Americans while BlackPlanet touts itself as the largest Black community online and AsianAve is a community connecting Asian Americans. Utilizing these networks, as well as other networks targeting specific groups (such as Glee, a community site primarily for the gay and lesbian community) can provide valuable insights into the particular needs of specific segments of a broader community.

While public social networks continue to dominate online activities, many companies are turning to private or "white-label" social networks to grow their brand and engage with a more definitive target audience. Private social networks offer complete control and flexibility to the creator, which can translate into unlimited research potential, particularly for research specific to fundraising campaigns. Many of the platforms used to create private social networks offer the same functions and features of popular public networks, including user profiles, instant messaging and much more. Private networks allow total oversight in terms of who can join, thereby enabling the creation of social sites to specifically targeted communities. Creating sites that provide unique social experiences is the key to attracting members and keeping them there. Knowing more about some of the most popular companies available for creating social networking sites will help you decide which one is the most suitable for your organization's research needs.

Custom Communities

Ning is one of the most widely used services providing private social networks, offering a user-friendly creation process and an abundance of feature options. The service offers custom design options and member profile pages. With Ning, you can choose to make your community public or private, approve members before they can join and moderate all photos, videos, chats, discussions and events before they are posted. Ning also allows you to create groups within your social network.

Taking a cue from the political realm, which shares so many similarities with the type of engagement that charitable organizations are seeking to establish, a report from the Emerging Media Research Council cited Scott Brown's win over democratic nominee Martha Coakley in the Massachusetts 2010 Senate Special Election as a victory for social media as well, due largely to Brown's aggressive social media efforts. Brown's social media campaign included a private network, called Brown's Brigade, which was set up through the Ning platform. At the time of the January 2010 report, Brown's Brigade had 6,000 member supporters of Scott Brown. The report also says, "The level of customization makes Ning an attractive choice for campaigns that want to develop an individual presence outside the bounds of Facebook."[5] This example and Ning's tools translate easily into the nonprofit platform.

ShoutEm is another popular design platform that allows users to create private, mobile networks that can be location based or aimed at specific groups. As with Ning, ShoutEm networks can be made public or kept private, and they also offer a multitude of

---

[5] "Social Media Use in the Massachusetts's 2010 Senate Special Election," *Emerging Media Research Council, Proprietary Member Briefing*, January 19, 2010.

customization options. Companies using ShoutEm include WE Harlem, Ranch and Rodeo and NFL Shouts. NFL Shouts founder Hussein Yahfoufi explains his decision to create a private network saying, "We decided we wanted to have a Twitter-like site but just for the NFL community. I really like ShoutEm because it has given us everything we needed to build our site without needing to do our own development. The mobile function is important to use. We've seen that the most traffic on NFL Shouts is during football games, so people can connect with each other at the ground."[6]

SocialGO allows the creation of private social networking with many of the same options available through Ning and ShoutEm. Personal profiles, blogs, forums and messaging tools are available. Multiple monetization tools are also available, allowing you to charge membership fees, host advertisements, sell products and display classified listings.

Metrics Old and New

The targeted access available through private, social networks will offer researchers the same qualitative insights gained through ethnographic methods on large public networks, only the information will be collected from a more controlled and definitive group of people.

Social media monitoring services are another useful tool for collecting quantitative research. There is an array of services available for anyone to research and record what is being said at any given moment about any given topic. These services provide an

---

[6] ShoutEm makes it easy for users to create private social networks," Total Telecom Online, March 3, 2010

advantageous way to find out what others are saying about a peer or competitor organization. More importantly, many of these services are available at little or no cost. There are many monitoring services to choose from, and it is a good idea to incorporate several methods into your research platform to compare results for more accurate conclusions.

The Google Alerts monitoring service is easy, fast and free; however, its reach is somewhat limited compared to other services. To use Google Alerts, you will need to enter the keyword search term(s) that you want to track and an email address where you want the information sent. By searching across the web including news and blogs, Google Alerts will then send you a daily email with a list of where your keyword(s) appeared on the web.

SocialMention.com is another free monitoring service that works similarly to Google Alerts, except that it gives instant results of your keyword search rather than a daily email. It also analyzes the data, detailing everywhere the keyword was mentioned, how often on average it was mentioned and the quality of each mention. More importantly for nonprofit fundraising campaigns, this tool also rates the sentiment behind each mention of the word you select, meaning it will tell you how many mentions were positive, neutral and negative. This can be a fast and efficient way to see how your organization is ranking among Internet users. That said, an April 2010 article from *PR Week* warns against placing too much weight on the sentiment-measuring tools offered by social media monitoring services, saying, "There is no substitute for real-life consultants who can expertly analyze the tone and implications of a comment and be in a position to act immediately if required."[7]

---

[7] Cathy Wallace, "Social media monitoring: Measurement—the experts at work," *PR Week (UK)*, April 2, 2010

Larger corporations and larger organizations may want to spring for monthly fees associated with one of several more precise and advanced monitoring services. Services such as Trackur, Radan6 (clients include Pepsi, Microsoft and Kodak) and Scout Labs (clients include Coca-Cola, Disney and McDonalds) offer more comprehensive tracking and analysis while also providing detailed information in dashboard-type formats. One of the most significant differences with the paid services versus the free services is that they will also rate the influential power (that is, an ability to influence the opinion of those who may be interested in your organization) of the site where your organization's name is mentioned.

It is probably safe to say that, like cell phones, social media has become a permanent part of our lives, with more and more users joining and participating in some form of social media each day. As social networking audiences continue to expand and philanthropic dollars continue to shrink, it becomes increasingly necessary for nonprofit and charitable organizations to participate in social networks in order to reach a wider and more engaged community. The interactions, conversations and general willingness to take part in online activities present research potential that is still in its early stages, so now is an important time to engage. It is also important to remember that social media should not be the only factor in a nonprofit's marketing and communications strategy. A research plan that integrates social media research methods with traditional offline approaches will give any nonprofit its best opportunity for fundraising success.

CHAPTER 5

Fundraising
Toolkit

W HILE EACH CHARITABLE ORGANIZATION is different, below are the major social networking platforms that nonprofits should consider as ways to travel through the constituent life cycle, from awareness and cultivation, to making the ask for volunteer or financial support, to stewardship and recognition, to a lifetime of engagement.

Nonprofit Facebook Fans

According to the Facebook group, Nonprofits on Facebook, more than 30,000 nonprofits use Facebook pages[1]. The Facebook Causes application reports that more than $5 million has been raised since 2006. This total has benefitted more than 150,000 causes.

---

[1] Nonprofits on Facebook page, 2010, http://www.facebook.com/nonprofits

For example, when the January earthquake struck Haiti, nonprofit organizations were uncertain how to proceed with social network marketing in order to raise relief funds. However, millions of dollars were raised when Facebook users across the world populated feeds with status updates urging friends to donate money through text messaging.

Important to remember is that a horrific natural disaster is not the only way to make Facebook a success for nonprofit organizations. As a standard part of fundraising, social networks offer a strong compliment to your existing efforts. For example, the World AIDS RED campaign utilized Facebook for its fundraising, and this platform quickly became the campaign's most viable channel for soliciting funds. In a blog post on Facebook, (RED) CEO Susan Smith Ellis wrote, "Our success is very much owed to the emerging world of social media that exploded, just when we needed it. Like social media itself, with (RED) the power is not so much in the act of one individual but in the incredible power of the collective acts of individuals. In just over three years, over 1.5 million people have joined (RED) via a range of social media" (O'Dell, 2009)[2]. Simply put, Facebook is a great way to spread the word through peer-to-peer communication, aka, "more feet on the digital street." And what charitable organization could say no to more frontline fundraisers?

---

[2] Jolie O'Dell, "Facebook, Google, and Twitter Unite for World AIDS Day Around the Web," December 1, 2009, http://www.readwriteweb.com/archives/facebook_google_ twitter_world_ aids_day.php

SNAPSHOT: AMNESTY INTERNATIONAL

Human rights organization Amnesty International includes more than 2.8 million members in more than 150 countries. With a community that large, Amnesty International relies on social media as a global communication tool. Facebook, Twitter, MySpace and blogs are used to inform and educate supporters about Amnesty initiatives and global human rights issues. A Flickr account enables members to post pictures from Amnesty-related events and a YouTube channel hosts videos profiling human rights issues and global news.

The organization has also demonstrated how social media can also be a useful fundraising tool. Outraged after learning that Shell's industrial activities in the Niger Delta were resulting in pollution in the area's drinking and irrigation water, the group sprung to action and organized a massive social media fundraising effort encouraging supporters among networks on Facebook, MySpace and Twitter, to help fund attack ads against Shell. The campaign exceeded expectations, with over 2,100 donations totaling more than £30,000 (approximately $38,292) for the London-based ad, marking the first time Amnesty International used fundraising to finance a campaign ad.[1]

The success of the fundraising campaign allowed Amnesty to purchase additional ads including one in a smaller publication and one to be featured on a van. Amnesty continued the campaign by engaging supporters well after fundraising goals had been met. They encouraged supporters to post pictures of themselves with the ad, which appeared in the "London Evening Standard" and "Metro," on Facebook and Twitter. They uploaded a GPS tracker on their website where supporters could track the movements of the van featuring the ad and then encouraged fans and followers to take pictures of themselves with the van as well.

[1] Rachelle Matherne, "Successful Fundraising through Social Media: Amnesty International," *Six Estate Communications*, May 18, 2010, http://sixestate.com/nonprofit/successful-social-media-fundraising-amnesty-international/

Charitable organizations can utilize Facebook in one of several ways:

- Create a Facebook page (or more than one, if your organization warrants this). Facebook is comprised of groups and pages. For the purposes of your nonprofit, create a page, opposed to a group. This is with good reason. Pages allow you to publish updates directly into the news feeds. This means a nonprofit can engage fans with a variety of media, including status updates, polls and videos. Pages also allow for an organization to analyze how fans are using the page by using the Insights Dashboard. The feedback provided by the Insights Dashboard allows an organization to adjust the methods they use on Facebook according to what is working.

- Utilize the Causes application. Created in 2007, Causes enables Facebook users to make a difference in the causes they feel most strongly about without ever having to leave their social network. The Causes application was founded on the theory that in a healthy society, any individual can participate in change by informing and inspiring other individuals. Facebook users can inspire others by telling friends about a cause, asking them to donate and just spreading the word about a particular cause. Clara Shih, author of *The Facebook Era* explains, "When users install Causes, a widget appears on their profile page featuring the nonprofit organizations of their choosing. Anyone who visits that person's profile can learn more about the charities, donate to the charities, or add the charities to their own Causes."[3] Thus far, this application is working. By the end of its first year, Causes had succeeded in raising more than $2 million.

- Provide content that is unique. While message consistency is always important, be cautious of simply duplicating what is found on your nonprofit's website. This defeats the purpose of using social media, which is designed to offer the value-add and a means of deeper engagement. Facebook content should be geared toward social media users. The content should be unique as well as thought-provoking to encourage reaction, comment and user insights.

- Frequently update the Facebook page. A Facebook page is designed to give users a glimpse into what the nonprofit does and is like. Use the various tools on the page to announce events, fundraising activities, meetings and other important activities. It also helps to engage users by posing questions seeking their feedback.

- Speak up. Facebook relies heavily on commenting, so provide ample opportunity for fans to do so. Track comments carefully. If, for example, you have plenty of fans, but zero comments, reconsider the value you are providing. While it may be that your audience is adequately engaged but prefers to simply consume,

---

[3] Clara Shih, *The Facebook Era: Tapping Online Social Networks to Build Better Products, Research New Audiences, and Sell More Stuff.* Boston: Prentice Hall, 2009

experiment with different approaches to information and conversation to gauge the effect. While no one is required to comment on every post made to a page, an utter lack of response may be an indication that you must rethink your content strategy or risk losing your fans. Further, even the occasional reply makes a great impression on a nonprofit's Facebook fan base and can serve to inspire additional comments and ongoing dialogue.

- Create an application, game or quiz. These elements can go a long way in developing an active and dynamic Facebook page. When deciding on a game or quiz, create one that users can engage with more than once. Make a nonprofit's application fun and exciting. This way, users will want to post it to their walls so that their friends and social network can use it as well.

- Creating a store or donation box makes it easy for fans to buy merchandise or donate money to a nonprofit's cause. Fans can participate without ever having to leave Facebook. More and more, we are seeing for-profit companies building e-commerce solutions within the Facebook platform, so charitable organizations would do well to follow suit. Again, before purchasing a bells-and-whistles, e-commerce solution, start small to gauge the impact.

- Purchase a Facebook ad. Facebook ads are usually placed at the right-hand side of a screen, are cost-effective and are an easy way to increase your fan base and visits to your nonprofit's site. Organizations can place ads based on the demographics and likes/interests they wish to target and can set a bid amount based on impressions or click-throughs, along with a timeframe for the ad to run. This approach can take niche marketing to a whole new level, and the great news is that unlike a costly advertising agency campaign, organizations can fine-tune elements in real time, and if they see an ad simply isn't working, they can turn it off or replace it on the spot.

Tweet Your Core Message

As nonprofit organizations begin to delve further into social media, Twitter should be one of the organization's primary channels. Because Twitter, which is a microblogging platform, allows no more than 140 characters per post, it is the perfect channel for promoting acute items of interest or information, along with sending core messages to a targeted base. Twitter can reach a large number of individuals with minimal effort. The top 100 Twitter users come from a range of industries, which includes the nonprofit sector.

To maximize your success with Twitter, try the following:

- Create a Twitter profile. This part is easy. It just requires a name, web address and a brief biography. The biography should be informative, yet catchy. Utilize well what little space is offered. With some basic knowledge of HTML coding, nonprofits can create a unique background. If this skill set is not available in-house, Twitter page design and implementation can be done at a nominal cost.

- Connect with other nonprofit organizations. It's simple: Following other nonprofits will allow an organization to build connections and earn support for a cause. It is important to engage in conversation with other nonprofits, reply to their messages and retweet them (e.g., forward their Twitter content) to your followers. Being active on Twitter can offer a great deal of visibility for a cause.

- Use Twitter to create a buzz around a nonprofit's cause. Twitter can be used to promote blogs and news on a regular basis. Most social networks have the built-in ability to network with other sites, so when you update your blog or Facebook page, for example, this update can feed automatically into Twitter. The more information an organization provides about its cause, the more likely it is to create excitement and involvement around that cause.

- Make tweets useful. Do not tweet gratuitously. Determine your "Twitter mix" or the content types that you will provide in advance. The general rule of thumb is an 8–2 mix. That is, eight of your tweets should be informational or entertaining (and related to your cause) and two of your tweets should be about what you really need (e.g., make a donation, volunteer, join the board). The trick is always to make tweets relevant. Create tweets that contain useful information that followers will be likely to re-tweet to their followers. Re-tweeting is an easy and effective means of spreading a message, but keep in mind, individuals generally re-tweet information that they find fascinating, humorous, heartfelt, or of value to their followers.

- They say a picture is worth a thousand words. This is especially true when it come to generating interest in nonprofit causes. Photos speak volumes when it comes to promoting a cause. Twitter may only allow for 140 characters, however, Twitpic.com, a Twitter "client" or Twitter application, allows organizations to add photos to their messages. In addition, sharing videos can help reach out to potential donors or volunteers. Photos and videos can trigger an emotional reaction and can inspire others to become involved by seeing firsthand the problem or issue, or the beneficiary of an organization's assistance. For example, The Mid-Atlantic Great Dane Rescue League uses Twitter to post photographs of the Great Danes they have rescued, rehabilitated and found homes for (Cohen, 2009)[4]. These photos told a powerful story to users—one that accurately defined what the organization stands for and that it is, indeed successful in achieving its mission. Users can see how their donations are put to use, which can be more valuable than any amount of repeat solicitations.

- Nominate the nonprofit organization for a Twitcause award (www.experienceproject.com/twitcause). Get people to vote for a cause by making individuals aware of the cause. If people recognize your organization and

---

[4] Lon Cohen, "26 charities and nonprofits on Twitter," 2009, http://mashable.com/2009/03/19/twitter-nonprofits/

believe it to be a worthy cause, they will vote for you. This, too, creates more awareness not only in the Twittersphere, but in the mainstream media.

- Use Direct Message (DM) when you get new followers. This Twitter feature can be set up to automatically deliver a message to your new supporters when they elect to follow you. The direct message allows for more characters than the 140-character tweet, and can be a great opportunity to foster additional involvement right away. You will want to be cautious not to present a message that is overly hyped or salesy—that is, a message that reads like spam. Rather, you might simply offer a message that says, "Thanks for the follow! For more information about how Charity X is helping to provide food for children in need, visit our website at …" The key is to utilize every opportunity to further engage an individual who opts in to learn more about your cause.

- Petition followers. Twitition.com allows nonprofits to create, sign and share petitions on Twitter. Organizations can ask followers to re-tweet the petition for their followers to sign. This is also a great way to get followers involved in a cause. In a similar vein, as introduced in Chapter 4, Twitter polls are a great way to ask a simple question and compile results based on your followers' responses. With so many Twitter clients (applications) available, polling can be easily included as a means of gathering user-generated opinion.

Link Up to LinkedIn

LinkedIn can provide a host of untapped potential for nonprofit organizations. This respected social networking site is comprised of more than 85 million professionals from 150 industries. Below are some tips for maximizing nonprofit exposure on LinkedIn:

- Make the organization visible. Based on your organization's policies and the comfort level of employees, ask everyone working for the nonprofit organization to create a LinkedIn profile. These internal, professional connections alone will create instant visibility for the organization.

- For those willing to participate, ensure that these employees include an extensive list of past employers in their profiles. LinkedIn alerts its members of past colleagues. A complete work history will enable the nonprofit organization to increase its social network. Individuals from the past will now have knowledge of this current cause.

- Use a signature that embeds the name of the nonprofit organization in it. This way, regardless of the message sent, employees of the nonprofit are getting the name and the cause into the digital space.

- LinkedIn profiles have a tendency to rank high on Google (Felten, 2009)[5]. This is great exposure for a nonprofit organization. To maximize potential exposure, make sure a profile is on full view and make public the profile's URL. To further increase success, link a nonprofit's LinkedIn profile on its website and use it when commenting on blogs.

- Create a LinkedIn Company Page. This newly created LinkedIn feature, which launched on November 1, 2010, offers organizations an even stronger way to market themselves via the LinkedIn community. As noted in the LinkedIn blog on the day of its launch, "Company Pages will enable companies to build their brand through network-aware recommendations, giving members rich, credible insights into how any given product (or service) is perceived by their fellow professionals."[6]

- Make other nonprofit projects known on LinkedIn. LinkedIn allows users to list blogs or websites. If a nonprofit has multiple websites or other social media pages, make them known. In order to increase Google rankings, write a short sentence or two regarding the organization.

---

[5] Katie Felten, "LinkedIn for nonprofits," 2009, http://epic.cuir.uwm.edu/entech/web/ symposium2009/handouts/LinkedIn%20for%20Nonprofits.pdf

[6] Ryan Roslansky, LinkedIn Blog, November 1, 2010, http://blog.linkedin.com/2010/11/01/ linkedin-company-pages/

- Be sure to use all the tools LinkedIn has to offer. Use the advanced search tool to find experts who possess the talents, experiences and interests that could be of value to the nonprofit organization. Post questions and responses to LinkedIn Questions and Answers. This can elicit attention as well as feedback from experts in the field and other nonprofit organizations and can serve as yet another conversation starter, while positioning your organization as an expert.

- Start a LinkedIn Group. This will raise awareness of the nonprofit's cause and increase credibility. As each member or individual associated with the nonprofit organization joins the group, a badge will appear on his or her profile. This badge will show affiliation with the group, build credibility and increase the organization's online presence. Invite volunteers, advisors and board members to be a part of this group.

Your Charitable Organization in the Blogosphere

With more than 100 million English-language blogs and growing, it seems as though every organization is blogging. If you are one of the nonprofit organizations that has not yet begun, add this to your "must-do" list. Blogs allow for significantly more conversation between the writer and the reader. Information can be relayed to many individuals quickly and globally. Blogging is one form of communication nonprofits must take advantage of in that it is one of the most efficient ways of casting the widest net to get your message to a broad population. Some important blog considerations include:

- Blogs can be used to link readers to breaking news about a nonprofit organization. Whether an organization made the local or a major national paper, a blog can release timely news to all its readers at a moment's notice. In addition, readers will not have to search for news on their favorite causes or nonprofits if the organization provides easy access to it through social media and linking. Every blog must have a means of sharing out content, such as an RSS feed, which gives those who wish to subscribe to your content the ability to have your information sent directly to them, rather than asking them to go to your web page for updates.

- Blogs can be used as calls to action. Bloggers can write posts asking supporters to send an email to Congress, attend a fundraising event, or even just check out the charitable organization's Facebook page. An organization will never know what its supporters are willing to do if it doesn't ask.

- Ask supporters to donate to a particular cause. A blog can be used to increase awareness of fundraising. Blogs can tell a story with passion and creativity that can captivate an audience. In addition, this story can be told briefly (most blog posts range from 250 to 500 words). All nonprofits that are using blogs to fundraise must be sure to include a "Donate Now" button that asks readers to contribute directly in the blog post. A "Donate Now" button provides quick and easy access for a reader to make a gift on the spot. If a reader has trouble figuring out how to donate, he or she will be less likely to donate and may simply give up. When asking readers to do anything, be sure to make the process of giving a gift, or becoming a volunteer, simple and convenient to use. Never make an individual have to work to support your cause.

- Nonprofit bloggers can use blogs to share stories, photos and videos from a wide variety of fundraising events. Bloggers should act as reporters and get the inside scoop on all events sponsored by the nonprofit organization. Blogs are a popular means of reporting back on events and can add to the appeal for the reader through the use of videos or photographs.

- Guest bloggers can share their expertise or experience working toward a particular cause. Nonprofits should seek out community leaders, activists, or educators to write a blog related to the goals of the organization. Adding well-known names to your blog can be a great way to spark traffic to your site and awareness for your cause.

- Blogging only about the nonprofit and its work is not always a good idea. Bloggers for the nonprofit will need to expand their themes. For example, if an organization is dedicated to children, a review can be written of a new children's book. The possibilities of what to blog about are endless. Bloggers should choose topics that are closely related to the organization, but creativity can go a long way in terms of sustaining and growing readership through interesting, value-added posts.

- Use a blog to highlight the positive. Blogs can be used to highlight press coverage. If a nonprofit finds itself in a magazine or newspaper, a blog can briefly discuss the story and then link readers to the original article. If the organization finds itself at the center of a news broadcast, be sure to get a copy of the story, particularly if it is televised. This can be posted as a video to the blog for a little something extra.

- Write a story about the nonprofit organization's success with the use of social media. Don't wait for someone to do this for you. Be sure to include the phrase "nonprofit social media success story" and the results will show especially on search engine results.

- Use a blog to conduct interviews. Nonprofits can post brief question-and-answer interviews on the blog page. These posts are interesting to readers and are simple for a charitable organization to complete.

SNAPSHOT: AMERICAN RED CROSS

For more than a century, the American Red Cross has been providing emergency relief efforts and promoting prevention and preparedness for areas affected by natural disasters and other catastrophes such as house fires. The American Red Cross has also become a leader in utilizing social media to connect with supporters, reach out to communities in need and raise funds.

The organization maintains a strong Facebook and Twitter presence, both of which are used to inform and educate the public about American Red Cross events, relief efforts and impending storms, floods or other disasters. A Flickr photo album enables users to upload photos of disasters and events and a Red Cross newsroom uses a constantly updated WordPress blog to update the public on impending dangers and upcoming efforts. The newsroom is connected to both Twitter and Facebook accounts. The YouTube channel provides video footage of areas in need of relief efforts and encourages viewers to donate funds as a show of support.

The American Red Cross redefined social media fundraising during its campaign to raise funds to provide relief efforts to victims of the January 12, 2010 earthquake that devastated Haiti. The organization launched a text-messaging campaign in which people were asked to send a text message to a specific number to have a $10 American Red Cross donation added to their cell phone bill. The campaign resulted in $32 million dollars for Haiti relief efforts. In an article for the U.S. edition of *PR Week*, Wendy Harman, social media manager for the American Red Cross revealed that the text messaging campaign was initially announced through their Twitter account before it went viral, saying, "All we had to do was tweet about it once. Twitter works great as an emergency notification tool."[1]

---

[1] Chris Daniels, "Nonprofits discover power of social media fundraising," *PR Week (U.S.)*, July 6, 2010, 18

Engage Through Flickr

Flickr is an extremely popular form of online photo-sharing. There are a number of photo-sharing sites (e.g., photobucket, Picasa) and many of the features that will be discussed for Flickr can be accomplished on other platforms as well. When selecting a platform, you don't necessarily have to choose the largest network. Your selection should be based on what works best to meet your objectives and the needs of your constituents.

Flickr is an online community that allows anyone to share and organize digital photos with family, friends, coworkers and individuals around the world. Like everything else social media, Flickr began as a means of sharing personal photos. However, it can be a powerful tool for nonprofit organizations in that it can help nonprofits to share photos online—another great content starter designed to elicit action in the form of comments, sharing, visiting your website, or taking action to become more actively involved. Some ways to get started include:

- Run a photo contest on Flickr. Nonprofits can use Flickr to engage supporters. Invite supporters to post their own photos. Supporters can be notified when new photos are added or if someone comments on the photo they have posted. For example, the March of Dimes conducted a Flickr contest. This contest asked people to photograph where they kept their spare change (March, 2010). Why spare change? A handful of change is often the weight of a premature baby at birth.

- Flickr can tell powerful stories. As the saying goes, a picture is worth a thousand words—this adage is borne out in the context of the nonprofit cause. Photographs can be used to tell the story of an organization as well as its mission, impact and ongoing actions. Flickr groups can be private or public and can be organized around a certain event, subject or theme. Encourage supporters to comment and give their feedback on the photos posted. Even a few photos can help to demonstrate the mission of a nonprofit organization and can help to increase awareness of your cause.

- Photos can help to promote events. Upload pictures from a fundraising event. In addition, encourage individuals who attended the event to do the same. Flickr can help an organization reach a much wider audience than if it just posted them on the organization's website alone.

- Flickr can aid in the launch of a fundraising campaign. For example, the Children at Risk Foundation's Reaching for a Star Campaign asked supporters to donate $10 to support its street kids' programs and to contribute photos to the group.[7] The photos and conversations around these photos proved to be a great success and donations poured in. Flickr is an easy means of launching a campaign. These campaigns are low- to no-budget, increase awareness and provide an interactive community for supporters and potential supporters.

- Photo-sharing can engage volunteers. Nonprofits can encourage their volunteers and supporters to share ideas, photos and stories. Nonprofits can benefit from the creativity of these individuals. Volunteers are always willing to help and it is amazing how quick they are to respond to this type of campaign.

- Through photo-sharing, Flickr allows supporters and potential supporters to appreciate the work a nonprofit has completed. This may cause sporadic viewers to

---

[7] Children at Risk Foundation, "Flickr Xmas Campaign—Reaching for a Star," 2009. Retrieved from http://www.carfweb.net/star_campaign.html

become regular visitors or perhaps even contributors to a nonprofit's cause. As the size of a charitable organization's Flickr group grows, the more exposure the cause will develop. Nonprofits just need to remember to stay on topic when sharing photos. If the cause is earthquake relief, nonprofits should be posting photographs of the area they are attempting to raise funds for. If the cause is feeding malnourished children, adding photos of the children in need will help make the cause more real and will generate more interest.

Position with Podcasts

Just about everyone has an iPod or an MP3 player. Nonprofits can take advantage of this technology. The only initial investment is recording equipment to capture a higher sound quality. Afterwards, the only cost in creating a podcast is the time of a nonprofit's staff. Podcasts can generate interest in a cause by literally getting the ear of potential supporters. A 2005 study by the PEW Internet and American Life Project found that more than 22 million American adults own iPods or MP3 players.[8] This form of technology is allowing nonprofit organizations to cash in. For those who don't use audio devices, any computer can enable users to listen to podcasts. In fact, many listeners prefer getting information in audio form so they can multitask by completing work as they listen. Some best practices for charitable organizations' use of podcasts are listed here.

---

[8] Lee Rainie, Mary Madden, "Podcasting catches on," Pew Internet and American Life Project, 2005, http://www.pewinternet.org/Reports/2005/Podcasting-catches-on.aspx

- Podcasts can enable leaders of nonprofit organizations to talk about the organization, its goals, mission, current happenings and the general state of the field or cause. This is especially beneficial if the founder or director of the nonprofit is a strong and inspiring speaker, as that adds a deeper dimension to the message.

- Nonprofit organizations can create short and informative pieces. These segments can focus on one issue at a time. The organization can use a voiceover by a narrator or host and mix interviews with people who have benefited from the services of the sponsoring charity. This creates a heartfelt message for supporters and potential supporters when they can actually hear stories about the good the organization has done.

- Use podcasts for updating information. A weekly podcast can update the happenings of a nonprofit organization. Weekly updates can also include commentary from experts in the field.

- Be creative when deciding on a plan for a podcast. Make the podcast enjoyable, yet informative. As with all forms of media, they are only what you make of them. Try new, innovative ways to engage a nonprofit's supporters. If a nonprofit organization finds itself with great feedback from a podcast featuring an expert in the field, continue to find more of these experts. If posting speeches does not work, you may want to consider trying something else. In addition, podcasts can be a great means of showcasing top volunteers or donors to your cause. With the advent of platforms such as Skype, recording an interview with an individual across the globe can be as easy as logging on to your computer.

- If a nonprofit organization attends conferences, speeches, or any form of presentation, these recordings can be used as part of a podcast. This will show individuals what the nonprofit organization does on a regular basis and how it is able to reach out to the communities and other organizations around it.

- If an organization already has a radio show, ensure that users can have access to the show as a podcast. This may be more convenient and can open up doors to new listeners. With services such as Blog Talk Radio, anyone can become a radio host, so if your content lends itself to this channel, or your audience can best be reached via Internet radio, you may wish to give this a try—it's another means of enlarging your social media footprint and the pervasiveness of your branding. Nonprofits should keep in mind that all messages should be delivered in a variety of media to ensure that supporters will receive the message. For instance, your podcasts should ideally come equipped with a printed online transcript so that the content can be read, printed and shared as text.

YouTube: The New "Must Have"

Nonprofit organizations have been using YouTube for years. According to ForeSee Results' 2010 Social Media Study[9], YouTube is the second-most powerful social network for consumer engagement. Consumer engagement is a vital component of generating interest in a cause, organization or association. Charitable organizations can use YouTube to reach out to supporters and provide an inside look into their causes in a manner that is immediately compelling. For example:

- Sign up with YouTube's nonprofit program. This program provides extra benefits to nonprofit organizations that choose to broadcast on YouTube. Benefits include branding capabilities, increased uploading capacity and call-to-action overlays. The call-to-action feature allows users to drive sign-ups, donations, website traffic and other types of response that require a user to take action. YouTube has become a powerful and highly effective means of raising cause awareness and funds.

- Nonprofits should link their cause with video annotations. Annotations are added to create interactive commentary and can also be used to link viewers to external sites. By linking users to external sites, viewers may be more likely to donate or volunteer for a cause, especially if they are linked to the nonprofit organization's website.

---

[9] ForeSee Results' 2010 Social Media Study, http://www.foreseeresults.com/

- If it is a struggle for a nonprofit organization to create its own video, YouTube has a volunteer program that will help an organization find a skilled videographer for its project. Plenty of YouTube video volunteers exist and are willing to help. With the rise in video literacy, a nonprofit may even be able to a find a volunteer who already supports the cause who is able to create the video.

- Search engine optimization (SEO) is also useful when it comes to getting a video to be viewed by the right audiences. All nonprofits should tag their videos, use appropriate titles and upload consistently to increase the probability of showing up in search engine results.

- Nonprofits should remember to keep their videos short in order to keep the interest of their viewers. Videos should be no longer than 10 minutes, which is on the longer side of short-form video. Ideally, one to three minutes works best. Videos longer than 10 minutes are likely to lose the interest of viewers, so don't try to pack in more than you should. Better to create a series of short videos, each focused on one specific message or point of support. If viewers lose interest, they are likely to miss out on important information that may be found at the end of the video, such as how to donate or how to volunteer.

- Avoid public service announcements (PSAs). Nonprofit organizations should be genuine. This is far more effective than a PSA. Genuine videos will generate more interest than highly stylized, overly produced segments. The real, "raw" video with minimal post-production can be more heartfelt and touching and will appeal to a wider audience.

- Encourage interaction with viewers. Organizations should allow individuals to post comments on the video. In order to create dialogue, the nonprofit should have someone responding to these comments. In addition, nonprofits should not be afraid of what their viewers have to say. Although they can moderate user engagement or disable comments, nonprofits should take what viewers have to say, learn from it and act on it.

Video Chat Touch Points

Video chat is an outstanding social media tool. Video chats allow nonprofits to make calls free of charge. Regardless of whether an organization uses video chat to reach out to supporters or for business purposes, video chat is a highly beneficial tool. Supporters can put a face to a voice and organizations can successfully make conference calls and save themselves money. In addition, as the world becomes more and more global, charitable organizations can connect in meaningful ways through video chat with supporters across the globe. While nothing beats being there, seeing one another in real time can be the next best thing. Elements to consider with video chat are as follows:

- Online tools such as Skype or Google Talk enable nonprofits to quickly share thoughts and ideas in real time. Be sure to experiment with these technologies ahead of time so as not to waste time learning these tools on your supporter's time.

- Video chats allow supporters to interact with each other and the nonprofit organization itself. Users can talk to supporters around the world at no cost. This allows for the exchanging of more ideas in a more timely way, along with the generation of increased awareness surrounding a cause.

- Communication via word of mouth is more social and personalized. Video chat adds the important dimension of personality to the person who is generating support and awareness on behalf of a particular cause. As the adage goes, people give to people, not to organizations.

- In the case of the charitable organization, gaining support for a cause often involves appealing to the human side of business. When appealing to the emotions of individuals, there is no better way to do so than talking face-to-face regardless of distance barriers. Face-to-face communication creates a stronger connection amongst individuals. This cannot be offered through any other form of media.

- Offering video chats to potential supporters gives them the opportunity to ask questions and feel comfortable about supporting a particular cause.

Going Mobile

Mobile fundraising has only been around for about five years, but has seen great success and an outpouring of donations from individuals who otherwise may never have donated. Here's how your charitable organization can "go mobile":

- Start with the option for text-message donations. This process is simple. The nonprofit organization begins by advertising the donation number to potential supporters. Donors send text messages indicating the dollar amount they would like to donate to the nonprofit organization, which generates a pledge from the organization and a check in the mail. Hundreds of nonprofit organizations around the world are taking advantage of the text-messaging donation campaign. Donation is easy for all parties involved.

  Easier than this is subscribing to a platform that enables the gift to be made directly through mobile. Companies such as mGive, while fee-based, can be well worth the investment and enable donations to be made in as little as 10 seconds. Note that cellular phone companies set different limits on the amounts of donations (the maximum limit was $10 as of the writing of this book) and international access to these types of applications is not yet available. That said, this can be a great means of donor acquisition at the lower levels of giving.

- Text-to-voice donations are a less commonly used method but an effective means of raising funds. This method is able to avoid the maximum text-message donation limit that is currently in place. A nonprofit advertises its designated fundraising phone number. When a donor sends a text message to the number indicating that he or she would like to donate, a staff member or call-center worker calls the donor back. During this phone call the exact amount of money donated is collected as well as the credit card information. Text-to-voice donations make raising more funds possible as well as creating a nice personal touch for the donor.

- Create a "warm-handshake" for potential donors through the use of a text message. Nonprofits can fundraise without collecting funds through mobile donations. The strategy behind this method is to keep donors engaged with the nonprofit and informed about the happenings of the organization. A nonprofit can send just a few text messages each month. This will help keep supporters of a cause excited and ready to donate when a nonprofit asks for its once-yearly donations. Maintaining a positive, non-fundraising connection with supporters is always smart strategy. Charitable organizations don't want simple check writers. Rather, they are looking for people who really believe in their cause and are willing to act to support it. Thus, across the board, social media means nonprofits must pay closer attention to value-added content than ever before.

- Nonprofits should take advantage of the smartphone craze. The number of individuals with the ability to connect to web applications through the use of their phones continues to rise. Depending on the type of website your nonprofit currently supports, it may make sense to develop a mobile-friendly version of your site so that it renders well for those who will access your content via a mobile device. With a "Donate Now" button, supporters can make their donations in the same way they would if they were sitting at home on their computers. Think of the possibilities at gala dinners, silent auctions, golf outings and other charitable events. The infamous, "I'd love to contribute, but I didn't bring my checkbook/wallet" could be a thing of the past.

- Phone applications can help with donations. If a nonprofit organization is willing to invest in a smartphone application, the application can be sold and the nonprofit can then collect the revenue. Thousands of nonprofit organizations have moved in the direction of smartphone applications and are generating revenue by selling their applications. One word of caution: Price your application accordingly. If you are offering something of value, then charge based on what the market will bear. Keep in mind that if you are merely providing a portal to access your site, these types of applications are generally presented free of charge, so know your objective and what to expect. That said, a compelling application experience can translate into many new supporters for a cause.

- Application purchases are another way to add to the use of mobile-phone fundraising. For-profit organizations sell digital goods for games in their applications. Nonprofits can take advantage of similar offerings, depending upon the type of smartphone application they have developed.

Like any other type of content, don't just develop to develop. Ensure that your application will add real value. Otherwise, save the development costs for something with a stronger return. Costs can rise quickly when building smartphone applications, so do your homework before you head down this path.

- Nonprofits can partner with a for-profit organization to create a sponsored application. This partnership can develop applications that promote business in exchange for donations. The concept of these partnerships is simple: Users purchase a product or service from a partner business, or purchase a product from a participating sponsor. The user earns personal rewards and the nonprofit receives donations from the sponsoring business. The best part about this type of partnership is that nonprofit organizations do not need to know much about smartphone applications and technology in order to take advantage of the increases in revenue that will result. In an era of corporate social responsibility, it doesn't hurt any charitable organization to ask corporations if they might be willing to partner on behalf of your good cause.

Nonprofits can also use mobile phones for micro-volunteering. Micro-volunteering allows volunteers to complete small tasks quickly. The task may be as simple as taking photographs. This task can be done while waiting for a bus or walking down the street to grab a cup of coffee. One institution of higher learning provides students with Flipcams so that they can videotape their experiences on experiential learning trips across the globe. Nonprofits who understand that individuals are busy and may not have the time to fit volunteering into their schedules can benefit greatly from micro-volunteering. This task requires no donations, yet allows an individual to get involved with an organization at his or her convenience using a mobile device that is ready at hand and frequently in use.

CHAPTER 6

Today's
Ideal Fundraiser

HIRING FRONTLINE FUNDRAISERS has always been a challenging experience for the nonprofit organization, its staff and its board of directors. These relationship-building roles of nonprofit fundraisers mark the cornerstone of an organization's efforts to meet its campaign goals, engage new prospective donors and reengage current and past donors.

Today's ideal fundraiser must possess all of the usual skills in terms of being able to serve as the representative face of the organization, tell the organization's story, present the mission in a manner that is compelling and ultimately, make the ask, secure the gift and return for ongoing stewardship and cultivation activities. In addition, another set of skills will give nonprofits an advantage— the use of social media marketing and promotion as part of the donation process—be it a specific campaign such as the annual fund or the nonprofit organization's ongoing fundraising efforts on behalf of more specific campaigns.

Not only are social media tools easy to use, but once fundraisers get the hang of them, they will realize the value in terms of free promotion of the organization, building the organization's brand, spreading the word about the cause or mission and increasing the amount of donations coming into the organization via these additional platforms. In short, social media can provide a charitable organization with more "feet on the street" of the online variety, so that peer-to-peer interactions can help drive fundraising and non-financial goals.

Before jumping into social media use as part of your fundraising strategy, though, it is important to realize that while social media can work tremendously on behalf of your organization, it can never replace those hard-won, long-term relationships you strive to establish on behalf of your cause. It is simply a set of additional tools you should use to broaden your current reach, bring constituents to a deeper engagement with your organization and to run a branding campaign for your organization in the online world. Conversations are taking place every day about your organization or organizations similar to yours in these online social networks. When you engage social media as part of your fundraising strategy, you are providing the platform to become a part of these conversations that are taking place, regardless of your level of involvement. Not only does this provide you with a place to communicate with your current and potential donors, but it also opens up the lines of communication so they can talk with you. Similarly, these spaces enable you to elicit quantitative and qualitative information from conversations they are having with other people and nonprofit organizations online. These learnings can inform your organization's approach to both friend-raising and fundraising.

Social media, as a fundraising tool, is a two-way street. In order for you to be able to ask for the donation, you first have to give. When you combine the social media world with the nonprofit world, the gift is typically in the form of information sharing. The possibilities regarding the type of information you share or how you use social media networking as part of your fundraising strategy are almost endless, but reviewing some of the ways that other nonprofits use social media can bring you up to speed on the right starting place.

How to Use Social Media to Your Advantage

The number of ways that you can use social media to help with your fundraising efforts is as infinite as an organization's level of creativity. When you are the person responsible for being the "face" of the fundraising efforts of the nonprofit, you are also the one responsible for figuring out how to integrate social media in addition to your standard fundraising events, letters and email campaigns. You should be able to draw inspiration from these examples and come up with some of your own innovative ways to roll social media marketing into the rest of your fundraising efforts. At the very least, the use of social media can help frontline fundraisers to combat some of the concern they routinely face with simply not having enough days in the year to make personal visits to core constituents.

Overcoming the Dreaded Friend Request

One point to note that comes up routinely: If you are a frontline fundraiser, determine in advance your personal social media policy. That is, if you receive a Facebook friend request from a donor, will you feel obligated to accept despite the fact that you would prefer to keep your personal and professional lives separate? If so, then have a standard response for these types of requests. The key here is consistency. If you friend one donor, you must friend them all and vice versa. No one wants to flat-out reject a constituent, so the situation can become immediately awkward.

The general response becomes simply to ignore the request and plead ignorance if asked. The smarter strategy is to offer an alternative engagement. Thank the donor or prospect for his or her offer, but note that you prefer to use your Facebook page for family alone. Instead, invite the individual to join you on LinkedIn or another professional network. Another option is to create a separate Facebook account that is specifically focused on cause-related friends. Direct the prospect to join you on this account where the two of you can engage with a community of cause-based friends. In sum, you'll never need to fear a request again once you have your personal policy in place. And you may find that you become the one doing the friending for this more personalized—but professionally based—interaction.

In terms of ways to engage your prospects, here are some powerful tactics to employ. If you are not the person responsible for updates, then ask your marketing and communications group if they might incorporate these strategies into their content mix.

- Upload photos of a fundraising event to photo-sharing websites such as SlideShare, Flickr or even upload them to the organization's Facebook page. You can also upload the photos to the nonprofit organization's website and share a link for the followers on social media networks to go to view all of the photos. This not only allows you to share photos with attendees, donors and more, but it also allows you to show prospective donors or those who did not attend the event precisely what they missed (the fun) by not attending. This gives them another chance to make a donation, contribute to the annual fund, or at the very least think twice about missing your next fundraising event. For those who cannot attend your organization's events because of geographic limitations, but still believe in your cause or the purpose of the event, uploading photos allows them to share in the event and go ahead and make the donation they would have made in person if they could have attended.

- Build excitement about your upcoming fundraiser with updates on your social media networks. Feeding small snippets of information about your event throughout the various stages can build excitement before the event takes place. In addition, sharing updates during the event allows others not able to attend the event to stay abreast of what is going on. After the event is over, you can update your audience with highlights. Providing details to your audience such as how much money you have been able to raise with their help, how much of your goal you have met, or how much more money you need to reach your fundraising or annual goal are just some of the updates for which you can use social media.

- In addition to the photos and text-based updates, videos and audio files are another sharing opportunity. You can upload videos of the staff of the nonprofit or even the end-result recipients that the dollars raised will benefit. While it may take someone 10 minutes to read a 500-word blog post, watching a five-minute video of the difference the event made in the lives of those who benefited from the fundraiser takes less time and can even be much more touching and emotional than the written word.

- In an indirect way of raising money, you can share blog posts or articles about your organization, its mission, or information that other sources are producing that relates to the goals and vision of your organization. While sharing useful and helpful information is not a direct ask, it builds credibility for your organization with its audience. A credible organization and one that is seen as the expert in the mission of your organization garners far more and faster donations than a nonprofit organization that does not hold this status in the minds of its current and potential donors. It also keeps your organization front of mind, so that when donors and potential donors consider their philanthropic priorities, they think of your cause, charity or need.

- Pose questions to your followers and use the answers as leverage for creating future fundraising programs, events or ways to meet their needs that are in line with the goals and mission of your nonprofit. For example, if a museum membership group enjoyed an afternoon-tea event fundraiser that took place years ago but was stopped for some reason, it may be time to bring back the event by asking followers if this might be of interest.

- Run a contest. Find a contest that directly relates to your organization. An art museum may run a painting contest, where the winner's piece will be used as part of the fundraising-campaign marketing materials, such as on invitations, brochures, letters, envelopes, rack cards, emails, on the organization's website and more. If you are in the process of rolling out a new educational program at the organization, hold a contest where naming suggestions for the new program are made and the organization staff (or even the other followers on the social media network) vote for their favorite name. Contests are always fun, interactive and great ways to collect the contact information of followers and contestants. They are also the perfect way to engage a social media network and then begin to grow it.

SNAPSHOT: POPE JOHN PAUL II HIGH SCHOOL

Pope John Paul II High School, located in Hyannis, Massachusetts, is one of few high schools to embrace the benefits of social media and integrate it as part of their school's online image. From the homepage of their website you can instantly connect to any of their social media platforms, including Facebook, Twitter, Flickr, YouTube and a WordPress blog.

The Twitter account and Facebook page include multiple posts a day communicating events at the school, inspirational quotes and local and national news stories that are relevant to both parents and students. The blog features fun guest posts from first-year teachers as well as freshmen students, sharing their experiences and life at the school. Flickr is used to keep photo albums of school events for students and parents to view and post comments on. The YouTube channel hosts video segments of various school events.

The Facebook polling application as well as Twitter's Twtpoll feature are also used in email blasts and newsletters for marketing and gathering statistical information. In an email to parents called "Countdown to Godspell" (a school play), parents were also invited via links to participate in a survey question about the play's composer, Stephen Schwartz. The poll was intended as something fun and social for parents reading the email to participate in. Links to both the Facebook and Twtpoll survey were provided; Al Catelli, Pope John Paul II's advancement and admission director and social media coordinator, determined that the Twtpoll survey garnered a stronger response than the Facebook poll.[1]

[1] Lorrie Jackson, "Social Media Case Study: Pope John Paul II High School (MA)," *Ed Social Media.com*, May 21, 2009, http://www.edsocialmedia.com/2009/05/social-media-case-study-pope-john-paul-ii-high-school-ma/

Because social media is an immediate way to share a multitude of information, incorporating social media strategies into your overall fundraiser strategy creates ongoing engagement between your nonprofit organization and its donor base, especially in between hardcopy letter-mailing campaigns or other offline engagement efforts. In the end, the more you can engage your current set of donors and reach additional prospects, the more tied in they will be to your organization and the more likely they are to continue giving, to start giving and even to increase their current donation amounts.

That said, also be cognizant of message fatigue. If you must use direct-mail or email to point your base toward your organization's social media sites, do so strategically. You will want to strike the right balance of content so that your donors and prospects do not begin to feel overwhelmed by the quantity of communications and thus less receptive to hearing from you. This again is where social media finds its strength in that these networks are predicated on an opt-in experience. Once your constituency has opted in, your job is simply to feed the networks to keep individuals engaged and informed. This becomes far less invasive—and far more meaningful—than the interruption-marketing techniques of the past.

Social Media is a Branding Tool

According to survey results released by Cone, Inc., 93 percent of Americans expect organizations to have a presence on social media outlets[1]. Of the core objectives that nonprofit organizations can use social media to accomplish, branding is one of them. When you use social media to tell the story of your organization and even to let others tell the story of your organization, you are branding the organization through social media.

In essence, your organization's brand is the reason it exists or provides meaning for the cause. Social media opens up conversations about your organization and allows your organization's story to unfold. When one of the children your organization supports lands a scholarship to go to college as a result of your fundraising efforts and that child is featured in a video sharing the story of how this scholarship changed her life, she becomes your organization's brand representative. This type of content sharing, which is a branding strategy in itself, jump-starts the credibility, trust and relationship-building of your nonprofit organization. Lisa Colton of Darim Online teaches nonprofit Jewish organizations about using social media. Colton notes that fundraising is about building relationships and that social media is a tool organizations can use to build these relationships.

She also shares that the organization should have a "face" behind the logo and brand because people want to know that when they leave a comment or interact with the organization's social media platform that they are "talking" to someone at the organization rather than the entity itself. With all of the information, resources

---

[1] Matthew O'Brien, Slideshare.net, 2009, http://www.slideshare.net/Blogster/social-media-marketing-and-branding-nonprofits-mint-social

and content sharing that social networks can provide, you are positioning your frontline fundraisers as the subject-matter experts on behalf of an organization or area of specialization within that organization.

The Importance of Online Cultivation

According to Fundraising Coach Marc Pitman, "One of our primary responsibilities is to engage donors and prospective donors in conversations. We often do that by giving tours of our facility or taking people out for coffee. These will always remain important tools. But some of my colleagues are saying the current economic downturn is making it more difficult to get appointments."[2]

Social media sites are making it much easier for nonprofit organizations to engage current and potential donors in conversations. Your prospects and donors are already having these conversations on social media outlets such as Facebook and Twitter, so when your organization engages in these channels, this creates a platform to become a part of a dialogue that is already taking place.

With millions of people using social media sites such as Facebook and Twitter to share photos, network and build relationships professionally and personally, when your organization participates in social media marketing, it is engaging your donors, board members and community constituents who are using social media platforms, too.

Engagement within social networks sends a powerful message to others when they land on your organization's page and see all

---

[2] Marc Pitman, "Twitter for Nonprofits and Fundraising," 2010, http://fundraisingcoach.com/free-articles/twitter-for-nonprofits-and-fundraising/

of the thank-you messages, words of encouragement, praise and more from your donors and the people your organization has been able to help through your fundraising efforts. That, as they say, is priceless engagement.

Ways to Use Social Media to Get More People on Board

If you are having an argument with yourself or trying to convince your board that in fact your constituents are using social media, consider that those ages 65 and older have doubled their usage of social media networks. Whether this age group is the audience for your organization is irrelevant because it simply goes to show that across demographics including age, gender and ethnicity, people are finding value in social media in one way or another. Using social media to get more people on board with your nonprofit organization and your cause is about knowing who your prospects and donors are and what they are looking for when they are engaging in social media use. Once you have ascertained this, then you can give them what they are looking for with your own updates, tweets and information sharing on your nonprofit social media platforms.

For example, the Association of Fundraising Professionals and the Association for Healthcare Philanthropy and publications such as the *Chronicle of Philanthropy* and *FundRaising Success* all have social media accounts with Twitter, Facebook and LinkedIn. Fundraising Coach Marc Pitman says you can engage these types of audiences by asking and by giving. When Pitman got stuck trying to come up with the postscript (P.S.) for a fundraising appeal, he reached out to his network saying, "Can you help?" Within minutes, social media followers responded with suggestions and one even went as far as to request that Marc send her his appeal letter, to which she made some suggested revisions, which made the letter far better than it was.[3]

On the flip side, nonprofit organizations are using social media outlets to share information, such as having members tweet about events while attending them. When professionals attend annual conferences and seminars, more of them are updating their social media profiles live while in the sessions. While interested parties of the professional group or organization may not be able to attend your fundraising event in person, they can certainly be kept informed of what is going on by following the updates on social media.

Choose Your Networks Wisely

While you do not have total control over who chooses to follow you on Twitter or becomes one of your fans on the organization's Facebook fan page, you do have control over the people you choose to proactively pursue. For example, if you have a donor who consistently supports your organization, you may want to go on to each of your social media networks and follow this individual on Twitter, friend him or her on Facebook and connect with this individual on LinkedIn. If you are uncertain as to the reaction, you might send an email first asking if this person is on these social networks and would he or she like to connect. Don't be offended if your supporter declines your invitation. Like you, this individual may have his or her own personal social media policy.

---

[3] Marc Pitman, "A case for Twitter, Facebook, and social media for nonprofit fundraisers," 2010, http://fundraisingcoach.com/free-articles/a-case-for-twitter-facebook-social-media-for-nonprofit-fundraisers/

In addition to connecting with existing donors in this way, you may also want to seek out potential donors and even other organizations and their members who have missions that are similar to that of your own organization. You will want to take a proactive and strategic approach to following and connecting with the top prospects or industry leaders in the areas that relate to your organization.

One tip for engaging if you are unable to interact with these individuals on a one-on-one basis is to start with LinkedIn. Review an individual's profile to determine which groups he or she belongs to. Try joining these groups, as you will then be connected to and able to network with all members of the group. By connecting to current and potential donors, and organizations and other leaders that can get your organization in front of the right people, you are laying the foundation for engaging these audiences with your messages. Remember, connecting is simply the first step. After you connect, you have to show them what your organization is all about.

More Social Media Best Practices

While using social media as part of your fundraising efforts is highly beneficial, there are also some pitfalls you will want to avoid. The first such misstep can be easily resolved by knowing your audience. For example, what may be appropriate to share with your followers on LinkedIn, which is primarily a group of professionals who are there to engage within this professional-career track of social media, is not what you may share on Facebook or Twitter, which have broader, more casual parameters in terms of content, tone and style.

Remember that what you share online is basically forever, even if you delete it. Obviously, this means that you will want to share only information, updates and content that highlight the organization, its representatives, its donors, volunteers and board members in the best light possible. Never post risqué photos, make suggestive comments, or provide updates that even hint at being questionable. If you have to question whether or not it is appropriate to share, then take the cautious route and do not share it at all. This goes for event photos showing individuals with drinks in hand. These may seem innocent enough, but you will want to avoid any problems down the road that may arise for the subjects or your organization.

Another pitfall to avoid in the use of social media in your fundraising efforts is not timing your updates appropriately. Proper planning when creating the marketing plan for your fundraising campaign can help you to steer clear of these types of mistakes. Be sure that your online and offline efforts are well-coordinated. It is embarrassing if you post about the annual campaign letter that went out in the mail and should have been received only to find that there was a delay from the printer and the letter has not even hit the mail. Instead of spending time raising money, these types of mishaps can leave you and your staff fielding unnecessary calls about a missed letter.

When you properly coordinate social media fundraising with other methods of raising the dollars your organization needs, frontline fundraising becomes slightly less of a challenging experience for the nonprofit organization, its staff and its board of directors. Since the relationship-building roles of nonprofit fundraisers are the foundation an organization relies upon to meet its campaign goals, to engage new prospective donors and to reengage those donors who have made gifts in the past, why wouldn't you use social media and all of the other available tools to ensure that your efforts are successful?

Ideally, the new breed of fundraiser must be social-media enabled, with an array of online tools at his or her disposal to engage constituents, maintain a conversation through value-added content and build stronger relationships along the way. Whether it is the annual fund, a special event, a membership drive, or a capital campaign, social media tactics are easy to create, simple to use, free and highly effective.

CHAPTER 7

Strategies
of Engagement

N MAY OF 2009, the Nonprofit Technology Conference in San Francisco conducted a survey on the nonprofit organizations that use social media marketing as a fundraising channel. Of those surveyed, more than 86 percent said they have social media accounts for conducting marketing efforts on behalf of the nonprofit. The most popular social media network was Facebook, with 74 percent of the respondents reporting use. YouTube usage came in second at 47 percent, Twitter at a close third with 43 percent, LinkedIn in fourth place with 33 percent, and MySpace at 26 percent.[1]

The more interesting fact is that at the time, the nonprofit respondents mentioned that their use of nonprofit social media marketing was mostly still in its infancy. Over 50 percent did plan to grow their use of the marketing channel. Close to 80 percent

---

[1] Mark Hrywna, "Social Networks Are Red Hot, Web Sites Are Diddlysquat," The Nonprofit Times, May 4, 2009, http://www.nptimes.com/09May/news-090504-1.html

said that one full-time staff person at the nonprofit would spend at least a quarter of his or her time devoted to handling social media networking and marketing.

Approximately 40 percent of survey respondents say they have been able to raise money directly from their efforts, with 29 percent saying they raised approximately $500 on Facebook within a 12-month period. The percentage of funds raised from other social media networks such as MySpace, Change.org, Twitter, YouTube, and LinkedIn were in the single-digit percentages.

Respondents admit, though, that their lack of ability to use social media networking effectively or the lack of a marketing budget for the organization are the two primary reasons for their lack of use or their inability to raise additional funds. At the time, the use of social media for most of the nonprofit organizations was less than a year old. Close to 94 percent of the organizations had been on Twitter for less than one year and on Facebook for six months to two years.

What may be the most fascinating statistic from the survey is the rank that nonprofits give for measuring success in using social media networking as part of their marketing strategy. Fundraising as a success measurement came in third place, while user-generated content came in first place as the most important metric for determining success on these networks. In essence, using social media networks comes down to engaging volunteers, donors and board members and adding new pipelines of support for the nonprofit organizations.

In 2010, social media marketing has a different look from the nonprofit perspective. Even though it is but one and one-half years later, Blackbaud fundraising software professional and social media expert, Frank Barry, notes that 22.7 percent of the time people spend on the Internet is spent on social media sites[2]. Barry also mentions that nonprofit usage of social media sites is not an objective that stands alone, but rather one that complements and integrates with other marketing efforts of the organization.

Ways to Put Social Networks to Work for the Cause

Marketing and social media experts alike seem to agree on one thing: Social media has almost endless possibilities in helping nonprofit organizations increase awareness of the cause, start a conversation with potential donors, volunteers and board members, raise money and cultivate new pipelines of support. Most also say that social media is still in the beginning phases of use for many nonprofits, but that it is already making a difference.

The Friends of Mel Foundation, which helps cancer patients, uses Facebook to promote the Mel's Magic campaign. Each month, the organization selects a different grassroots organization that shares the mission of helping others with cancer. Friends of Mel promotes the chosen organization on Facebook and Twitter by letting its fans know the organization is a Mel's Magic grant recipient. Mel's has 3,160 Fans and 307 active monthly users, with a Facebook page that is just two years old.

Since tight marketing budgets are a reality that most nonprofit organizations share, social media helps these organizations overcome this because the basic platforms are free. Minus some of the time it takes for the marketing or development manager to

---

[2] Frank Barry, "Nonprofit Social Media Primer," August, 2009, http://internet.blackbaud.com/atf/cf/%7BA1758E1C-C5FF-4DC3-89ED-DC2343EF76A3%7D/8-09.BBIS.SOCIALMEDIA.WHITEPAPER.PDF

plan social media campaigns and implement them, social media marketing does not eat away at any of your budget. If this sounds intriguing, it should. Here are just some of the ways that nonprofit organizations are using social media in their marketing efforts. These examples should help you to draw inspiration on how to inject social media into your charitable organization.

The Moyer Foundation is an international nonprofit working to help children in distress. The foundation utilizes an integrated marketing approach, using social media tactics in conjunction with its existing marketing strategy. Tactics include regular postings on Facebook and Twitter, real-time updates and tweeting during events and ongoing engagement with a growing fan base. The social networks and content encourage donations and allow the foundation to provide updates and information on fundraisers and events.

For example, Nology Media and The Moyer Foundation participated in USA Today's #AmericaWants Twitter contest to win a full-page advertisement in the newspaper. The Moyer Foundation came in 16th place and gained a great deal of exposure over the four-day period, along with some very influential tweeters helping to spread the word. The Moyer Foundation's followers tweeted 932 times, which amounts to one tweet for every three followers.

Domus Kids, which is a nonprofit with a mission to help homeless and disadvantaged kids in Connecticut, had a yoga studio adopt the nonprofit on Facebook. The yoga studio regularly follows the organization and spreads the word about Domus' work via the yoga studio's Facebook posts and their participants now donate to the organization.

SNAPSHOT: BROOKLYN MUSEUM

The Brooklyn Museum, located near Prospect Park and the Brooklyn Botanic Garden in Brooklyn, New York, is one of the oldest and largest art museums in the United States. While, the 560,000-square-foot building houses a diverse collection ranging from ancient Egyptian to contemporary art, the Brooklyn Museum's social media presence could be defined as cutting-edge. With a social media strategy that includes a strong presence on Facebook, Twitter and YouTube, the common thread throughout the Brooklyn Museum's social media presence is that it is personable and conversational, ensuring a connection with each follower and fan.

The Brooklyn Museum has also created an innovative socially networked membership program, 1stfans, which is an interactive membership program bridging an online and offline museum-membership experience. In a personal communication August 27, 2010, Nitasha Kawatra, membership director, explained the program, writing, "1stfans is a $20 membership that targets an audience who values both face-to-face experiences and benefits online." She explained that one of the primary offline benefits is access to Target First Saturday events where members can interact with one another, as well as artists and staff. Attendees can then photograph and videotape their experiences at the events and then share them with other members online. Kawatra also pointed out that one of the biggest online advantages to the program is exclusive access to the Twitter Art Feed, a protected Twitter account hosted by a different guest artist each month. Some of the artists in the past have included Duke Riley, Joseph Kosuth, Jonathan Lethem and Mike Monteiro. Kawatra added, "1stfans are primarily Brooklyn-based (with these demographics strongly resembling the museum's regular membership), though 1stfans has also succeeded in generating international membership. In an effort to respond to and engage this faraway audience, initiatives have been implemented to generate a sense of belonging outside the walls of the museum. For example, 1stfans posted a video welcome on YouTube for 1stfans' members who couldn't physically be present at First Saturday events."

Capturing New Audiences

Social media networks are similar to opening a new door to a new audience. Yes, many of your donors, volunteers and board members are on these networks and these are the individuals you may already be reaching with your other marketing channels. In addition, there are plenty of other potential donors, volunteers and future board members that are lingering on these sites. And, these are individuals that you may not otherwise have the opportunity to attract if you didn't run into them or they didn't run into you on a social media network.

Not only do you have the chance to broaden your reach with new individuals, but you also have the opportunity to connect with other nonprofit organizations and for-profit businesses that align with the mission of your organization. By following these entities on social media networks, you can learn how they are successfully using social media to further their cause. In addition, you can get in front of the audience that is following the organization, which is the same audience that has the potential to have an interest in your charitable institution's cause.

Communicate with Subscribers/Followers/Friends

Going back to the basics of marketing, you already know that once you identify prospects with an interest in your charity, it is then time to start communicating with these prospective volunteers and donors. Social media marketing is one additional way to communicate with your prospects, attract new leads and convert leads into donors, volunteers and others involved with your organization's cause.

Event Announcements

While events vary based on the type of nonprofit you're involved with, generally speaking, charitable organizations tend to host numerous events at points throughout a given year. While some of these events may have a specific fundraising purpose, others may have an educational focus, or a stewardship and recognition rationale, as a means of publicly thanking those volunteers and donors who have contributed time and talents on behalf of your organization. Whatever the reason or purpose for the event, social media outlets serve as a great way to spread the word quickly and easily. You can use the update feature on social media outlets to announce the event, collect responses, share additional information about the event and ask your followers to help you inform a broader audience through their networks.

Educational Tidbits

Ideally, social media marketing should be integrated with other marketing methods and techniques, so you can mix and mingle social media with what you are already doing to promote the organization. If you publish a new blog post on the organization's blog, post an update using social media and include a link that directs the follower to the post on the blog. When you send out your bi-monthly e-newsletter for the organization, include icons for each of your social media accounts so that subscribers to your newsletter can follow you on these additional communication channels. Remember, the more you can engage an individual, the more loyal he or she will become and the more likely you are to turn this individual into a supporter, a donor, a volunteer or a board member.

Useful Articles

Your organization may write and share its own set of informational articles. Informational articles aren't necessarily about your organization, but may share information that is related to your cause. Try sharing a combination of your own articles and articles from other sources so that you can build credibility with your audience as a resource for useful information.

Attract Joint-Venture Partners for Cause-Related Marketing

A joint-venture partnership occurs when your organization forms a partnership with a business for a specific purpose. For example, American Express joined efforts with a group raising money for the restoration of the Statue of Liberty in the late 1990s. American Express promoted the partnership by encouraging consumers to apply for a credit card. For every application received, the credit card giant would donate a set amount of money to the restoration project. While this particular venture did not have social media marketing at its disposal, now you can use social media networking to both find joint-venture partners and promote the partnership in a manner that is mutually beneficial to both organizations. This is also known as cause-related marketing—when a nonprofit and for-profit organization team up for a mutually beneficial goal.

Broaden Your Organizational Reach

With small and sometimes non-existent marketing budgets, it is hard for nonprofit organizations to buy mailing lists and run a direct-mail campaign to attract new members or donors. Nonprofits, however, can accomplish the same goal using social media outlets to broaden their reach and quickly increase their number of followers.

LIFT is a nonprofit organization combating poverty and expanding opportunity in the United States. LIFT uses Facebook, Twitter, YouTube and Flickr consistently and maintains a Scribd (a social reading and publishing site) account for uploading interactive documents to its website. A few tips and tricks LIFT has picked up using social media:

- Social media is as much about sharing as it is about self-promotion. If fans don't feel like they're having a conversation with the organization or learning something new, posting doesn't do the organization any good.

- Social media isn't necessarily a job for an intern. With a public platform that reaches thousands of people, you have to be careful that the tone, image and frequency of posts are consistent and send the right message to your audience.

- Link your Facebook and Twitter pages so that you don't have to double-post, but be aware that Facebook and Twitter users interact in very different ways. Facebook users tend to like seeing images, videos and links, but don't want to see hashtags or @ symbols in posts as is common with Twitter.

- Use video.

- Try an online grant competition. LIFT competed for $250,000 in the Pepsi Refresh Project in the inaugural month of competition and that drove hoards of new people to its Facebook, Twitter, YouTube and website pages. Even if you don't ultimately win the grant, your supporters feel like they are actively participating in something, they can contribute to the financial health of the organization without emptying their pockets, and it's basically a free public relations campaign.

How to Connect the Social Media Dots

Once you realize what a powerful tool social media is, the next step is to plan your attack. Similar to any marketing effort, social media marketing requires you to create a plan for how to approach social media marketing so it is aligned with the values of your organization. Experts who help nonprofit organizations to integrate social media marketing into their marketing efforts agree that planning to implement a social-media marketing strategy breaks down into a five-step process.[3]

Step 1. Set objectives. Determine what you expect to get out of using social media marketing and make sure that the objectives you set are aligned with the overall objectives of the organization. One objective may be to establish a following of at least 5,000 people on the organization's Facebook page. Another objective may be to roll out a special fundraising campaign to raise $10,000 for your cause.

---

[3] "5 steps to planning your social media," The Nonprofit Times, http://www.nptimes.com/newsletters/instantfundraising/instantfundraising06242010.htm#sub2

Step 2. Make someone accountable for the role. Social media marketing can be a full-time position. Even if your nonprofit organization cannot afford a full-time staff person in the role, it should be a role that takes up a significant portion of the marketing manager or development director's time. As the LIFT organization experienced, handing this role to an intern who did not grasp the tone and messaging the organization needed to employ for its audience, the organization saw a decline in its social media efforts until someone in the organization who understood the importance of these factors took over these important social media efforts.

Step 3. Engage in social media marketing circles and network groups that relate to your nonprofit. Get involved in these communities so that you are reading what your constituents are saying and what your fellow nonprofit organizations are doing to engage audiences. Be it donors, volunteers, potential board members or other parties who are interested in your organization, if you listen to what they are saying in these social media platforms, you can hear loud and clear the types of information they are seeking. You can then answer the call when using social media for your own organization and accomplish your goals at the same time.

Step 4. Set up your social media accounts. Once you gather information on how to build a presence for your organization in the world of social media marketing, you then have to take the steps necessary to put the profiles together and get up and running on social media networks. Spend time considering and writing the information on the organization's profile to include words and phrases that your target audience would be using to find an organization like yours. Again, reviewing information on other productive nonprofit organizations can help provide a guide as to what information you should include and information you may want to avoid. While you will never want to copy another organization's profile, you can certainly mimic the good parts and model your organization's profile after another successful charitable organization.

Fill out each profile on each social media network completely (partial profiles send the message that an organization may not be fully committed), upload a logo or photo for the organization and review the profile for grammar issues, spelling problems or missing information before posting it live for all of your donors and prospects to see.

Step 5. Stay connected. Once you start using social media marketing for the nonprofit organization, you have to stay engaged. This requires the person in charge of the social media marketing to regularly post content, to respond to messages, comments or questions and to monitor the conversations that are taking place about the organization. One of the biggest mistakes nonprofit organizations make is not regularly monitoring their social media accounts. The entire premise of social media networking is the two-way interaction it provides. If your audience is engaging you but you are not engaging back, this defeats the entire purpose of using social media in the first place.

For example, the South Florida SPCA uses social media marketing in a variety of ways to produce both online and offline results. Some of the ways the organization uses social media marketing are to:

- Drive traffic to its website by referring visitors from social media networking to the resources available on the nonprofit's website.

- Post pictures of available horses. Everyone complains that the website is not updated fast enough, so the organization uses social media to invite volunteers to post their own photos of the animals and their comments. It takes the work off one person in the organization and allows updates on a more frequent basis.

- Seek donations. The organization requires regular donations and creates messaging to remind its supporters. It uses Facebook to post its more urgent needs.

- Recruit volunteers. Many volunteers hear of the organization through the news or by searching online. By reading the information on the Facebook page, individuals can learn more about the organization to help them decide to volunteer. The positive comments of others who are already volunteering encourage new volunteers to register.

- Seek adopters and foster homes. Many inquiries about the horses available for adoption and foster care come through the Facebook page and the organization can share adoption information and instructions through Facebook.

- Educate the public in animal welfare. The South Florida SPCA shares information and posts from other organizations, as well, to be a resource for all things animal-welfare related. This encourages followers to keep returning to the Facebook page.

- Inform the public of activities. The South Florida SPCA uses Facebook to bring timely news and events to its followers and it is a faster method than any other method the organization uses. The organization can announce information before the news breaks, which provides the organization's followers with an inside scoop.

- Promote fundraising events and ranch activities.

As the stories throughout this book affirm, social media marketing is taking the nonprofit world by storm. The great news is that there is no set limit on how successful your social media networking and marketing efforts can be. In a similar vein, there is also no one methodology or set of tactics that will ensure success. Social media marketing is not a stand-alone marketing effort. It is one additional online method for engaging interested parties in a way that is complementary to your other marketing efforts and its success is ultimately reliant upon quality content presented with consistency.

As the increase in participation in the 2010 Nonprofit Technology Conference indicates, more and more nonprofit organizations are riding the powerful wave of social media marketing. Social media marketing is changing the way that nonprofits interact with donors, volunteers, board members and fellow nonprofit organizations. This form of interaction is opening new channels of communication and is cementing the relationships between the organization and its constituents. This solidifying of relationships is ultimately leading to more donations, contributions, volunteer hours and commitment to the organization and its cause.

CHAPTER 8

Communications

COMMUNICATION IS A KEY FACTOR in the success of any nonprofit or charitable organization. Strong communication between the organization and its supporters is imperative for advocating issues, raising awareness, promoting causes and fundraising. The most important aspect of communication is maintaining two-way conversations between organizations and supporters to establish loyalty and ensure that contributors feel like they are a part of the organization beyond simply writing checks and attending events.

Your Social Media Case Statement

While it used to be that the marketing and communications arm of the charitable institution was solely responsible for producing that high-gloss, content-rich, photo-heavy case statement that displayed to the most engaged constituents your organization's critical campaign needs, today's case statement becomes more of a fluid exercise. In addition to producing the print and online versions of the case statement proper, social media provides a new opportunity for charitable organizations to present their case statement in more meaningful and focused ways.

Thus, the case statement becomes a living, breathing, dynamic representation of the evolution of a campaign in progress. An organization's use of video, beneficiary testimonials, guest blogs from those who have already donated to the campaign, podcasts featuring specific elements of a fundraising campaign, educational lectures presented via webinars and video blogs—all of these become the tools your organization can use to advance past the stagnant, hard-copy case, and into a world in which campaign needs, goals and points of progress are brought to life in a manner that is far more meaningful and far more effective.

Social Media Integration

Beyond the case statement, integrating social media into conventional forms of communication is one of the most effective and efficient ways to achieve this. The networking capabilities and global reach of social media will strengthen communication efforts and enhance supporter engagement. In the same ways that businesses are capitalizing on the use of social media to drive traffic to websites, strengthen relationships with customers and build brand recognition, nonprofit organizations can accomplish these same goals by building social media into their communication strategies.

Nonprofit communications once relied solely on phone calls and direct mail to reach supporters, but the Internet brought a new form of communication with the advent of email and electronic newsletters, also known as e-newsletters. Social media has since redefined communications and, according to a Nielsen report, February 2009 marked a significant shift in how people are spending their time online: statistics revealed online users spent more time on social networking sites than on email. The report also disclosed that from 2008 to 2009 email enjoyed a 9 percent increase from a time-spent perspective, while time spent on social networking sites increased 73 percent, enabling it to catch up to and then exceed email.[1] However, a study from Epsilon in conjunction with ROI research revealed that 87 percent of online users in North America use email as a primary form of communication to 4 percent who identified social media as their leading communication tool.[2] By integrating email and e-newsletters with social media, organizations will utilize all of the dominant forms of communications, which will only serve to increase their base of supporters.

Email and E-newsletters

Email and e-newsletters should serve as the foundation of any nonprofit organization's communication portfolio. The key to successful communication is using multiple channels and social networking sites are part of the package. A survey of nonprofit organizations by VerticalResponse, Inc., found that social media and email marketing was expected to increase significantly

---

[1] "The Global Online Media Landscape: Identifying Opportunities in a Challenging Market." Nielsen Online, April, 2009, http://nielsen-online.com/emc/0904_report/nielsen-online-global-lanscapefinal1.pdf

[2] "Inside the Inbox: Trends for the Multichannel Marketer; Epsilon's Global Consumer Email Study," Epsilon, June 2009, http://www.epsilon.com/pdf/Global_Consumer_Email_Study_6_4_09.pdf

among nonprofit organizations from 2009 to 2010. Half of the organizations surveyed reported an increase in email marketing in 2009, and 73 percent planned to ramp up email marketing efforts in 2010.[3] In personal communications on September 7, 2010, Jordan Viator, interactive communications manager at Convio, Inc., an Austin, Texas firm providing technology and consultation services to nonprofit organizations underscored the importance of using multiple channels to reach an audience, noting, "Social media elements will continue to become more standard to include in emails. As with any other communications channel—direct mail, email and so forth—multichannel marketing is more effective than a single channel. Because of this, the new standard of including social media elements in emails continues to help increase awareness of organizational social channels while also starting to build relationships in another channel as audiences visit the various other channels (social networking sites)."

Growing a useable and substantial email list is crucial to the success of any email marketing campaign. Finding ways to encourage supporters to opt-in and subscribe to email messages can be a challenge for businesses and nonprofit organizations, but nonprofits have a slight advantage over for-profit businesses because people generally are more inclined to request email about causes they care about, as opposed to messages that are simply trying to sell them something. In addition, there are built-in databases within many nonprofits including universities, hospitals and many industry-based organizations. Still, acquisition of current email addresses remains an ongoing dilemma for most nonprofits. The primary methods used by charitable organizations to obtain email addresses are sign-up sheets at events and sign-up forms on

---

[3] "VerticalResponse, Inc. Surveys the State of Non-profits in America; Reports on Trends in Marketing Channel Use Across 2009 and 2010," *Marketing Weekly News*, February 20, 2010, 40.

the organization's website. A website should have a sign-up button, prominently displayed in the same location on each page to link users to a sign-up form from anywhere on the site. Social networks, such as Twitter and Facebook can be used to promote the sign-up form and link fans and followers, who may not be subscribers, back to the site to sign up for an e-newsletter and email. Facebook can also be used to grow an email list without requiring people to leave the social networking site. Nonprofits can create an email sign-up tab and add it to their organization's Facebook wall.

Basic HTML and an embed code from the email provider service is necessary to do this but it can be a huge timesaver for people who may want to sign up but don't want to leave Facebook to do so. Viator noted that, "Numerous clients using the Convio platform have taken advantage of integrating email sign-up forms directly into a Facebook tab. In turn, they are beginning to see significant email list-building results from directly within Facebook, never having to ask constituents to leave their social experience."

SNAPSHOT: MARCH OF DIMES

The March of Dimes, a leading nonprofit organization promoting healthy pregnancy and infant health, has been successfully using various social media platforms for different organization efforts for more than two years. In addition to a Flickr account, where members can post photos from events and a YouTube channel featuring stories, videos and celebrities promoting March of Dimes, the organization also hosts three separate Twitter accounts, targeting different demographics of the March of Dimes community. The main account, March for Babies, is used to promote events and the annual walk that takes place in various cities. The account March of Dimes is used to post pregnancy health tips and other relevant news while Baby Tips is for new parents seeking tips and advice for a healthy baby.

The March of Dimes in collaboration with public relations firm Barkley PR has also leveraged a Facebook fundraising application to raise money and donations from the community. In an article for *PR Week*, Mike Swenson, president of Barkley PR, explains the importance of social media in nonprofit fundraising efforts, saying, "It is a great channel in terms of micro-giving—enabling supporters to ask a wide audience to donate a small amount of money. For nonprofits, it's a way to open up their story to a new audience who, at least for the moment, can't write the big check."[1]

The March of Dimes enables participants in the March for Babies fundraising walk to download a fundraising widget to their Facebook page, which tracks their goals and progress while allowing friends to donate directly though their Facebook page. In the same *PR Week* article, Patricia Goldman, vice president and chief marketing officer for March of Dimes, revealed that 56,000 of 71,000 Facebook fans were using the fundraising widget, adding, "You can no longer do major fundraising events without the involvement of social media. People are much more willing to post something on their social media accounts than send out 500 emails. And from a fundraising perspective, Facebook reaches a broad platform of people."[2]

[1] Chris Daniels, "Nonprofits discover power of social media fundraising," July 1, 2010, *PR Week (US)*, 18.

[2] Ibid.

Incorporating social media elements into e-newsletters is another necessary component of multichannel marketing. Adding links within an e-newsletter is an essential tool for communicating events and happenings within an organization to audiences who don't regularly visit the website. Creating newsletter content that is engaging, informative and interesting is paramount to a successful e-newsletter communication platform. The email study conducted by Epsilon found that irrelevant content was the primary cause for users to unsubscribe from permission-based email programs and receiving emails too frequently followed close behind.[4] As important as it is to include links to the organization's social network profiles, there is also a reciprocal benefit of social networks in that conversations, questions and discussions created by supporters can be used to develop content in the e-newsletter. This will encourage supporters to participate in discussions via social networks and make them aware that their voices are being heard, ideas are being listened to and concerns are being addressed. Viator agreed with this concept, adding, "As new discussions are started, comments made and popular items shared, organizations can use this as actual content in e-newsletters. What better way to share what your supporters are interested in than by actually taking what's been proven to be popular content and include it in mass updates?" Integrating social media into an organization's e-newsletter serves to increase the value of the newsletter to the organization's support network.

Peer-to-Peer Appeals

Including social media links and share links in an e-newsletter will broaden communications beyond the organization's support base by encouraging recipients to share information with friends on their social networks. Viator echoed this concept, saying, "Integration of social media links and sharing into the e-newsletter is important. This helps organizations expand their voice and mission by having supporters share their messages on their behalf. Ways to do this include a standard 'connect with us' toolbar at the end (of the

---

[4] "Inside the Inbox: Trends for the Multichannel Marketer; Epsilon's Global Consumer Email Study," Epsilon, June 2009, http://www.epsilon.com/pdf/Global_Consumer_Email_Study_6_4_09.pdf

newsletter) to simply connect with the nonprofit in social media, and perhaps more effective, including 'share' capabilities on specific items and content to allow people to actually share granular content within their own personal networks."

Once an email list has been established and a campaign has been implemented, it is crucial to know how well communications are being received, what percentage of recipients are actually reading the content and how many are clicking on links to social media sites and other page links. Using link-shortening services that offer analytics reports can help organizations track click-through rates and gain a better understanding of what content audiences are most interested in. Link-shortening services, such as bit.ly, Cligs, TinyURL and the shortening service offered through HootSuite (a handy Twitter and social media dashboard for managing multiple Twitter accounts and social networking platforms), among others, provide in-depth analytic research to show how many people are clicking on particular links. For instance, if an organization creates a link to its Facebook page in the e-newsletter, it can use a URL-shortening service to create the hyperlink rather than the actual Facebook page URL. This will enable the organization to review click-through rates and other data associated with the specific shortened link.

This information can be used to assess and improve communications, as well as take note of which are the most popular links. It will also help to provide a clearer picture of how many email subscribers are actually opening the email. Viator elaborated on this, saying, "By using link-shortening services, the raw number of clicks can be measured and thus broken down to see, overall, how effective any set of social links perform next to each other. Also, increasingly more services and technology companies are offering heightened tracking services, such as query links added to hyperlinks that can break down where traffic came from and what types of action were taken to show at a more granular level the effectiveness of social media activities."

Nonprofit organizations can also take advantage of the reciprocal benefits of both communications platforms—email and social media. Using tie-ins between the two, organizations can encourage supporters to open email and participate in social networks. For instance, an organization can use Facebook and Twitter updates as teasers for an upcoming e-newsletter. Providing content cliffhangers will encourage more subscribers to open and read the email. Similarly, the e-newsletter can be used to encourage supporters to participate in surveys, post photos on Facebook and Flickr, or whichever social media platforms an organization wants to focus on.

Annual Reports

Annual reports are an important and necessary form of communication for any nonprofit organization. They are essential to maintaining and expanding an organization's existing network of supporters. Annual reports should communicate to donors how the organization is allocating funds, detail the success of the organization's events, educate supporters about issues facing the organization and inform constituents about all of the organization's efforts in championing its cause.

As social media continues to play an increasingly more significant role in these areas, including social media statistics will continue to become an essential part of the annual report. Communicating how social media efforts are expanding the organization's reach and helping to promote advocacy issues, events and other goals is necessary to include in an annual report so that donors, volunteers and other supporters can gain a better understanding of how social media is impacting the nonprofit's mission.

Social media is essentially a grassroots tool for communication and fundraising, allowing donors at all levels to support causes they care about. As previously cited, when the American Red Cross launched a text-messaging campaign to raise money for relief efforts in Haiti, it enabled anyone with a cell phone to contribute by texting a message to a specified number to make $10 donation, which would be included in their cell phone bill. The campaign raised $32 million for relief efforts.[5]

Rather than targeting a handful of large donors, the Red Cross harnessed the power of social media to tap into a global audience. It is important to every donor to know that they were a part of that contribution, thus the significance of including social media efforts in an annual report. This will ensure that donors at all levels feel like they are a part of the organization and will further enhance their engagement in future social media efforts.

Photos are usually included in annual reports, as many people are drawn toward images more so than facts and figures. An organization may benefit from using photos for its annual reports that have been submitted to Flickr albums and Facebook pages by supporters, donors and volunteers. Utilizing photos from constituents will strengthen their sense of belonging to the organization and encourage them to participate in photo-sharing via Facebook, Flickr or other photo-sharing networks.

Several nonprofit organizations had already begun to include social media efforts and statistics in their 2009 annual reports, including the American Red Cross, well before the 2010 catastrophic

---

[5] Chris Daniels, "Nonprofits discover power of social media fundraising," *PR Week (US)*, July 1, 2010, 18.

earthquake in Haiti. In its 2009 report, the American Red Cross dedicated a page: "Connect with Us on the Web, Any Time, Every Day." The content revealed, "...we realize that to remain relevant and ensure our growth, we need to be on the forefront of new technology. We've fully embraced social media. Our followers on Facebook reached 90,000 last year, and our president and CEO, Gail McGovern, has blogged to let our supporters know what was happening at the Red Cross in real time."

The report went on to inform supporters how their support via social networking helped them raise money, saying, "Thanks to thousands of supporters the Red Cross won 26 percent of the votes in Target's Bullseye Gives on Facebook campaign last year, in which 10 nonprofits competed for a piece of Target's $3 million donation. You cast 75,000 votes for the Red Cross, earning us $793,942 for our humanitarian services."[6]

In its 2009 annual report, the March of Dimes revealed how social media was helping to spread awareness of issues associated with premature birth, saying, "During November, Prematurity Awareness Month, thousands of moms joined the fight for preemies on our website, in local communities and on their blogs. With 13,200 blog posts, March of Dimes moms reached more than 3 million readers, helping spread the word on the serious problem of premature birth."[7]

In her opening letter of the 2009 Annual Review, Ingrid E. Newkirk, president of PETA (People for the Ethical Treatment of Animals) explained how the organization had leveraged multiple social media platforms to reach a global audience and further

[6] "American Red Cross 2009 Annual Report," 2009, American Red Cross, 20.

[7] "March of Dimes Annual Report 2009," 2009, March of Dimes, 2.

the organization's cause, writing, "Thanks to our adept use of the Internet for activism and outreach, we achieved several milestones in this realm in 2009—amassing more than 450,000 animal rights friends on Facebook, attracting more than 65,000 followers on Twitter, becoming the fourth most subscribed-to advocacy group on Youtube.com and exceeding 5 million views of our heartbreaking videos on YouTube.com. Our blog ranks in the top one-quarter percent of all the blogs in the world!"[8]

The Social Media Ask

Fundraising is critical to the success of any nonprofit organization and in the ways that people once relied on phone calls and face-to-face fundraising, social media has created an outlet that enables an organization's supporters to reach out to their own networks of friends and family to help raise money for causes they care about. Referring to the American Cancer Society's Choose You campaign, which encouraged women to pledge $5 toward their personal health goals and then ask their social networks for donations, Alison DaSilva, executive vice president for Cone, the marketing firm responsible for developing the campaign said, "We like to think of it as 'friend-raising.' Nonprofits need to remember that social media is, first and foremost, there to help people be social and share information."[9]

As the most popular social network with a diverse user demographic, Facebook has easily become a primary source for

---

[8] "PETA Annual Review 2009: President's Message," 2009, PETA, http://features.peta.org/AnnualReview/

[9] Chris Daniels, "Nonprofits discover power of social media fundraising," *PR Week (US)*, July 1, 2010, 18.

social media fundraising activities. Organizations have capitalized on Facebook's fundraising potential in a number of ways. Facebook's Causes application is one of the earliest and most actively utilized fundraising applications on the social networking site. The application allows users to show their support for a cause by joining the cause on Facebook and donating through the application. They can display the cause on their profile page and allow friends and family in their network to join and donate. It is relatively easy to start up a cause and even smaller organizations have found it to be useful for fundraising.

According to a post on the Nonprofit Technology Network website, "The Love Without Boundaries Foundation created a cause despite being small, entirely new to Facebook and having no paid staff. They have raised over $150,000 to provide medical care for Chinese orphans and even have 10 babies they call the 'Facebook babies' because their surgeries were made possible by donations through the cause."[10]

Many organizations including the March of Dimes have enabled supporters to add fundraising widgets to their Facebook profile pages to allow friends and family to donate without leaving their social network. Patricia Goldman, vice president and chief marketing officer noted that more than 56,000 of the organization's 71,000 Facebook fans have installed the fundraising application and generated donations with it.[11] Other organizations have developed Facebook game applications to promote causes and raise funds. In 2008, the Nature Conservancy, in collaboration with a service provider, developed a popular Facebook application, (Lil) Green

---

[10] Effective Fundraising with Facebook Causes," June 18, 2009, http://www.nten.org/blog/2009/06/18/effective-fundraising-facebook-causes

[11] Chris Daniels, "Nonprofits discover power of social media fundraising," *PR Week (US)*, July 1, 2010, 18.

Patch, in which users maintained virtual gardens, invited friends to plant patches, sent virtual plants to friends and helped tend the patches using sponsored items. The campaign engaged 6.3 million people and saved more than 70 million square feet of rain forest in Costa Rica.[12]

Communication efforts used in conventional fundraising efforts include events, direct mail solicitation, foundation grant solicitation, in-person solicitation, telemarketing and planned giving (e.g., bequests, trusts, annuities). In today's convenience-driven society, social media should be a factor in any fundraising proposal.

With millions of people across the globe engaging in social networks, they can provide vital fundraising resources to benefit nonprofits of any size. Communication teams and fundraising strategists should collaborate with one another to assess how social media can be leveraged in a fundraising or advocacy campaign. They should work together to determine how to engage their support base in a way that will inspire and motivate them to recruit their personal networks of friends and family to contribute and participate in fundraising activities. In the planning stages, it may be determined that only one social media platform is needed, while other campaigns may require multiple social media channels.

Aside from getting supporters to add widgets (small pieces of computer code that enable users to embed an application within their blog, page, etc.) or cause buttons to their Facebook profiles, organizations should also review ways in which other social media efforts might be used during a fundraising campaign. For instance, if a fundraising effort is planned around an actual (as opposed to virtual or online) event, an organization may want to use a photo-sharing site such as photobucket or Flickr to allow donors and supporters

---

[12] Ann Moravick, "Nonprofits Look to Shake Up Their Social Media Game," *Promo*, June 7, 2010, http://promomagazine.com/viralmarketing/news/0607-nonprofits-social-media/

to upload photos of the event and encourage engagement with the fundraising campaign. As important as a fundraising campaign is to earn actual revenue for the organization, it will quickly fall short of its goal unless an organization is able to retain supporters for the duration of the campaign and ensure that they feel engaged. Using social media to communicate fundraising goals, real-time progress and achievements from within the organization's social media support base will help to achieve this.

CHAPTER 9

Special
Events

Incorporating Social Media into Your Next Event

F
ROM "SAVE THE DATE" announcements to feedback
surveys, event planning for nonprofits is not what it used to
be. In many respects, it is a great deal easier. What used to
be pages and pages of lists, color-coded pages and endless updates
that never inspired any real confidence, is now a smart and efficient
opportunity to engage your membership and attract potential
members in a coordinated, more streamlined way.

Lists Update Themselves. Depending on the type of event, private
or public, using social-media enabled platforms for managing event
invitations and responses, means that participants will update your
list for you. In fact, your guests will expect to be engaged in the
process. They will offer comments that keep you informed of their
opinions and suggestions.

Make it Easy on Your Guests. They Will Reward Your Organization. The convenience of an online silent auction or live-streaming an event is paramount to attracting those who otherwise might not be able to attend in person. Another crowd pleaser is event photos. You can show your guests how much fun past events have been by posting photos on a photo-sharing site or even to your organization's Facebook page. After the event, guests will enjoy instant "fame" when they see photos of themselves posted. They can also have the option of posting their own photos. As noted earlier, if you have any concerns about guests who may not appreciate the fame of a public photo, ask in advance, pull photos of those who decline to be featured and have media releases handy if need be.

Feedback. After the event, you can ask participants to provide feedback using an e-survey application such as SurveyMonkey. This can provide your organization with invaluable analytics and insight into making future events more successful. You can also reach out to attendees via Facebook by asking them what made the event a success, or what aspects didn't appeal to them.

Best Practices. What are the best techniques and strategies for a successful event for your organization? How will you determine which approaches and methods will be most effective for the size and scope of the activity at hand? How will you engage your membership to help your organization grow and similarly, how will you connect with volunteers, members and organizational leadership?

Event-planning professionals will all agree that the key to any successful event is organization. Using social media to prepare for your next soiree will help keep you and your guests organized while adding time-saving value and efficiency to your organization's bottom line.

Because social media is interactive, you can encourage your guests to provide comments, ask questions about the event, or even to invite other attendees. This takes a large burden off of you and your staff, while at the same time, helps build relationships with current or potential donors, members, or leadership and provides you with valuable feedback from those you are targeting for fundraising.

You may find that your participants are not only expecting to be engaged, but that they prefer to be contacted in a way that is more convenient for them to spread the word about your event or respond to you directly.

SNAPSHOT: JEWISH COMMUNITY FEDERATION OF CLEVELAND

The local chapter of the Jewish Community Federation in Cleveland, Ohio, provides events and information supporting the Jewish community in the area and they are one of few chapters successfully tapping into the full potential of social media. A 2009 article for "Crain's Cleveland Business," reported that two years earlier the only use that the Jewish Community Federation of Cleveland had for Facebook was just to help its Young Leadership Division find new recruits.[1] Realizing the diverse age demographic of Facebook users, the organization now uses its Facebook page to recruit volunteers of all ages, promote events and connect with the Jewish community in Cleveland. In the same article, Daniel Blain, senior vice president for the federation, indicated the organization would expand its use of social media tools, adding "(Social media) is clearly a growing area of interest for us."[2]

As of August 2010, the federation's social media presence has grown to include a Twitter profile complete with frequent posts about community events relevant to Cleveland's Jewish community. A WordPress blog features news stories elaborating on events and happenings within the community and a YouTube channel featuring videos of events and a look inside the federation.

Another unique aspect of the Jewish Community Federation of Cleveland's social media presence is a Jewish CLE application, which is a free mobile application for users to connect to the community from anywhere at any time. The application features a community calendar, community directory and an interactive map. The application also enables users to view event photos, connect to the federation's social networks or view videos from the YouTube channel.

[1] Chuck Soder, "Social media become key tool for nonprofits; Sites help groups raise funds, promote their causes," Crain's Cleveland Business, December 7, 2009, 5.

[2] Ibid.

Facebook is obviously the most common tool for sending out "Save-the-Date" notices and event invitations. Depending on your event, you may want to control the privacy and security of your guest list; whether or not attendees can or should invite others or share information about the occasion. Facebook will allow you to select privacy controls when you set up the event, but a simple statement, such as, "An RSVP on Facebook is not an official response. You must purchase a ticket to be admitted" can also help you control your guest list.

Twitter can become another indispensible tool in the social media toolkit, and one method is through the use of the #hashtag. A hashtag is a keyword with the pound sign "#" in front of it. An example would be: "#CBCGala" or #WildlifeHH. Use the hashtag whenever communicating about your event via Twitter, Facebook, LinkedIn and so forth. Encourage your guests to use it, too. Not only does this instill a sense of community, but it also gives you the tools to determine the level of interest in your event and what people are saying about it. TweetDeck (another useful Twitter and social media dashboard) is one of many free applications that allows you to "cross-pollinate" your posts to Facebook and Twitter so you will only have to post once to Twitter and the other two will update themselves. Hashtags are a great way to search on a keyword to view the entire stream of like conversations pertaining to your topic or event.

Typically, for a high-dollar event such as a gala, fashion show or silent auction, your guest list will be limited to the spending level of attendees who can afford the price of the tickets. You may want to encourage those on your list to share the invitation with their friends and colleagues. This also gives you the opportunity to capture the names of potential donors and in particular, the next generation of leads and interact with them online.

Event Staging and Promotion

Some organizations use other online tools, such as Eventbrite to organize their events. This has come full circle as Eventbrite allows users to share information about the occasion on Facebook, LinkedIn, and they now have a "Tweet Button"[1] with which guests can share with their friends the event information. Eventbrite also allows those attending the event the convenience of updating their online calendars by offering a downloadable feature for Outlook, Google, Yahoo and iCal. A word of caution: This could increase attendance dramatically, so be prepared if you are planning an invitation-only affair at an intimate venue, this may not be the strategy you will choose to implement. This strategy would be ideal for those who are looking to cast a wide net for members and supporters.

---

[1] http://blog.eventbrite.com/new-tweet-button-comes-to-eventbrite

Your organization could use this as a tool for a holiday party, or a benefit concert or show, or even a happy-hour event. The immeasurable benefit of having a larger-than-expected turnout, along with accurate, up-to-date contact information for all of the guests—those who came and even those who didn't—goes without saying. This would be a great opportunity for your organization to prospect potential donors or new members.

For a more intimate affair, a standard Facebook invitation, along with a note directing your guests in the proper RSVP procedure will help you in controlling how many and which guests you'd like to invite.

In the case of a silent auction, guests may log in to a Flickr account, prior to the event, to assess the items on which they will be bidding. You should be in control of who has access and when items are available for viewing. It is generally the practice to have the actual bidding done in person, at the event, rather than online. Guests will typically want to examine more closely the items on which they plan to make an offer. Naturally, paintings, clothing, jewelry and the like all need to be inspected and "held up to the light" for an investor to make an educated guess on the item's value.

In some cases, however, bidding can be done online. If you were auctioning off items such as gift certificates to be redeemed at hotels, spas, stores and boutiques, or amusement parks, you would simply provide links to the appropriate websites and ask participants to bid during a certain timeframe. Websites, such as Online Charity Auctions,[2] specialize in hosting online auctions for nonprofit and charitable organizations. Online auctions are a fun and cost-effective way to raise funds and engage members as well as spark the interest of potential members. While these websites have the capabilities

---

[2] http://www.online-charity-auctions.org/

to auction tangible items, it is not recommended. Shipping costs and buyer's remorse can make an otherwise fun event turn sour. It is best to stick to gift certificates and group packages when using online bidding.

Facebook, Twitter and Listservs are all good ways to promote your auction. Whether live or online, social media is an effective resource to communicate to your supporters—and to those who haven't heard of you yet—the items you are offering, the date and time, and the reason or cause for which you are raising funds. Consider tying all of these resources together with a #hashtag. An example would be, #SilentAuctionSpaday, thus alerting those following your organization that they can and should use the designated hashtag for that particular item. The hashtag will allow you to track and index the level of interest in the item or items up for bid.

Photos Can Communicate

Whether your event is a silent auction, a gala or a dinner, or even a happy hour, your guests will love to see the photos of themselves, their friends and other guests. Uploading them directly to your organization's Facebook page should be done with consideration of guests' privacy. A more secure and organized way to share event pictures is sharing the photos on an online photo management resource that provides customized security and privacy controls to help you organize photos from your event. Participants can comment on the pictures and share information with each other. It can also be cost-effective. Encourage attendees to take their own pictures of the event and post them online to a predetermined photo-sharing account.

This is a cost-cutting activity that limits the services of a professional photographer, while helping to steward membership engagement and participation. Starting a "Digital Documentation Committee" ensures a thoughtful process going forward, while building relationships and leadership involvement. With so many amateur photographers and even more photographs, many organizations opt to have a Photo Contest. Photo contests can inspire commitment to the organization as well as provide an opportunity for members to be involved and interact with each other. To further member involvement, have event attendees and general members vote for their favorite photo or photos online for a period of time before announcing the big winner.

You don't have to limit photo contests to tie in with events. Depending on your organization, you may want to offer a photo contest to express a part of your mission or further your cause. This can be similar to the online auctions in that the contest costs very little to produce, but will have the benefit of having a positive impact on membership and will foster the desire of others to become involved as well.

Most important to every successful event is the participation and graciousness of the guests. A quick and well-thought-out "Thank you" to everyone who attended your gala, dinner, auction or happy hour is always appreciated, if not expected. It's a little tricky to send a "Thank you" note to all of your guests on Facebook. Be sure that you have created an "Event" on Facebook and have not, instead, hosted the event by your "Page." If your Page has created the Event, you will not be able to message the guest list.

If you have, in fact, created an Event, then you can message the guests as long as the entire list [Attending, Not Attending, Maybe Attending] does not exceed 5,000. If you've gone over 5,000 guests, the best solution might be a "Thank You to All" posting on your organization's Page. It's not as personal, but you can always create a list of guests you must thank, in addition to the general post. If your event is that large, it is probably most useful to use a resource like Eventbrite for your invitations and thank you notes. This service will allow you to message all of your guests, with no restrictions.

Online and Blended Events

The Tweetup

If you follow groups on Twitter, you may have received a tweet inviting you to a Tweetup. The Tweetup (or Twitter meet-up) takes the powerful community of Twitter followers to the next level of engagement with your organization by arranging a real-time networking event.

Some rules to remember if you are hosting a Tweetup are to ensure that you have selected an appropriate venue based on your budget (read: a friendly networking setting as opposed to a crowded bar or a noisy setting). Determine how many people you would ideally like to have in attendance and have a cut-off number clearly listed on the event invitation. The last thing you want to do is to create an overcrowded, ill-planned event. Likewise, you'll want to assure that you have a minimum number of guests so that the event is engaging and worthwhile.

To this end, use email and sites such as Eventbrite or Meetup. com to manage invitations and details pertaining to the Tweetup. Good speakers and good food are an important part of a successful event, so you'll want to consider these factors as well. If you will have a cash bar, note this on the invitation so that guests know what to expect.

Some examples of organizations who have held successful Tweetups include LATISM (Latinos in Social Media), a 501(c) 4 "nonprofit, nonpartisan organization dedicated to advancing the social, civic and economic status of the Latino community" (LATISM.org), that does a fabulous job of using a network of channels to engage Twitter followers and those associated with LATISM through real, social networking events across a broad geographic region, thus proving out the value of online media, which manifests itself in offline impact.

Webinars

For those unable or unwilling to engage in the more meaningful face-to-face events, webinars can help to bring individuals together for an online event based on a common interest or cause. These online, web-based seminars can become the jumping-off point for supporters, volunteers, future board members and donors. While it is harder to capture a real-time group (e.g., research shows that most individuals would rather download a white paper than sit through a webinar), if the topic is sufficiently compelling, the audience will materialize.

This can be used effectively for areas of fundraising such as planned giving. For example, your donor base might find real value in a webinar on the topic of "The Importance of Planning Your Will" but may not wish to express this interest publicly to the organization. In this case, a webinar, which offers a level of anonymity for the user in that he or she can consume the content without being "seen" by the group, might be the perfect means of providing information that will eventually compel a donor to contact the organization about plans for a bequest.

Likewise, with volunteer training for phon-a-thons or fundraisers, a webinar can bring groups of people together without the expense of items such as facilities rental, refreshments, or travel. In fact, the presence of webinars can encourage busy individuals to participate at a greater level given the built-in convenience of the online environment.

The important takeaway with online or blended events is knowing your target audience and then trying a few experiments on a smaller scale (e.g., core volunteers, executive board members). Events of this nature that are successful can then be scaled for the larger population.

New Forms of Follow-Up

You'll also want feedback after the event. There are several directions you can take for post-event feedback. SurveyMonkey[3] and Constant Contact[4] supply online surveys that are sent to out to each attendee via email or through a link posted on your website, with customized questions specific to your event.

SurveyMonkey is a good place to start. It will help you drill down to your guests' preferences and the specific issues they would like to see addressed. SurveyMonkey is a good basic program that will help you to get an overall picture of your event. The general rule of thumb is to keep the questions simple and concise.

At times, it may be appropriate to post the results on your website ("90% of participants agree, Nonprofit Gala was a success!"), but, in

---

[3] http://www.surveymonkey.com/

[4] http://www.ConstantContact.com

general, the data is best used for internal planning and development of best practices.

In addition to online surveys, Constant Contact also has an email marketing feature. It has slightly more functionality than SurveyMonkey and provides over 40 different design templates. Constant Contact also allows you to schedule surveys in advance and import contacts.

While SurveyMonkey and Constant Contact are efficient ways to receive information and reaction from attendees, several organizations have had success with integrated web tools such as FormSite[5]. FormSite allows you to build forms directly on your organization's website. It's a cost effective and user-friendly way to capture data and feedback.

Some organizations have found that that an open comments section on their website or Facebook page encourages attendees to share their ideas and concerns about the event. You can help get the ball rolling by asking provocative questions (e.g., "What did you think of the size of the crowd at Nonprofit Gala?") The more specific the question, the more thoughtful the responses will be. Try not to ask "Yes or No" questions. As participants are commenting, be sure to respond to them in real time. This will keep the discussion alive. You will also want to monitor the comments for inappropriate content. Obviously, the open comments approach will not garner scientific data as with practical online surveys, but you will certainly get a feel for the general mood and interest level. The open comments approach can also be more labor-intensive than an online survey. Ultimately, you will have to decide the best way for your organization to expend its resources.

---

[5] http://www.formsite.com/

As it is in life, timing is everything. Common sense will dictate a rational approach to mapping out your event timeline, but you will want to optimize your rollout by scheduling invitations, updates and surveys to coincide with prime user time. Most people check in on Facebook during the early evening hours, to "catch up" with the day's events and to keep track of events, friends and family. Consider timing your postings to hit the users' "newsfeed" at the end of the day.

Asking for feedback might be better timed for later in the evening or over the weekend, when users have more time to sit with the question and compose a thoughtful response. Beyond the time of day, you should also focus on the time of year. You will want to determine when is the best time to engage your membership, your potential pool of members and your leadership.

If an anniversary or remembrance that is central to your mission is coming up soon on the calendar, mention that occasion in your posting, thus capitalizing on the interest and involvement. You can provide an opportunity for your leadership to engage prospective members around the occasion, while you steward the relationships with current members.

Be Accurate. With so much information flying about, you don't want to clog the information arteries by disseminating misinformation and then having to correct it. Resist the urge to post something quickly. Take five minutes and review what you intend to post, *before* you hit the "share" button. This seems like an obvious rule, but you'd be surprised how many people ignore it.

Be Concise. Brevity is the soul of social media. Be direct and to the point. A provocative headline is essential. Decide what you want to say and then decide when to say it. For events, you need only the reason for the occasion, date, time and venue. The rest is incidental. You want to avoid spamming and too much information. Do not get mired in your hopes and dreams for the organization or the event. That is what your website is for.

Start Small. It would be unwise to start using social media for the very first time while planning your annual gala. Start small. Host a happy hour or networking event using the Facebook event feature. Test out surveys, forms of follow-up and online auctions. Remember, this is new to some of your membership as well. Part of engaging with your members is realizing that you are all part of this experience, together.

Different Events Require Different Strategies. Gala events will require a different social media strategy than an online auction or a happy hour. You may want to cast a wider net for the online auction or happy hour, while the gala will garner fewer attendees with a higher qualitative value. Keep in mind, fewer attendees doesn't necessarily mean a lesser level of interest. You can live-stream the high-dollar event, or upload edited video of the event afterward, on your website and post the links for your followers on Facebook and Twitter.

Whether you decide to host a gala event, an online auction, or a small gathering, it is important take a moment to pause and reflect on what you have accomplished. In the excitement of beginning a new project and applying new tools—sometimes with expectations set too high—we don't anticipate that with our new "powers" to communicate come new and unforeseen possibilities that things won't go as perfectly as we had planned.

Be prepared to talk about these mistakes and begin to reflect on the successes. Take time to debrief and ask the tough questions that might lead you to new insights.

Below are some of the top questions you should ask following your event:

1. What ideas worked well?
2. What goals were accomplished?
3. Which specific tools worked the best?
4. Did the event fall short? In what way?
5. What could you have done differently?
6. What surprises came up during the event?
7. What insights did you gain?
8. What ideas did you use that worked well? Which didn't work so well?
9. How was membership engaged?
10. Were there conflicts?
11. Were relationships made stronger?
12. Were you able to attract new members? How many?
13. Were there people or perspectives missing from this project that you would include next time?
14. What areas of focus would you spend time on for your next event?
15. What were the most challenging aspects of the event?
16. How can you transfer what you've learned from this event to other events or projects?
17. What caused the most problems for you and how will you address that in planning future events?
18. What are the unanswered questions?
19. What would you like to learn more about that would help this (or other projects) in the future?

20. What is the takeaway? What did you learn from this?

Incorporating a social media strategy into your organization's event planning is not a "one-size-fits-all" process. Each organization has special needs and unique qualities that make for thoughtful policies and procedure discussions. Design social media protocol around your organization's unique event planning needs and build upon what you can learn from each event and the feedback of your guests.

CHAPTER 10

Social Media
Stewardship

S TEWARDSHIP IS A VITAL COMPONENT within the life cycle of a donor-nonprofit organization relationship. In the past, nonprofit organizations went through (and still do, to a large extent) extensive offline methods of providing stewardship to the individuals and groups that contribute to the nonprofit organization and keep it going. When the Internet entered the scene, many nonprofit organizations saw a whole new world opening up with regard to ways of thanking its donors, collecting donations and promoting the organization, its cause, its events and simply staying front of mind with its audience. Social media networks, such as Facebook, Twitter and LinkedIn have become important tools and extensions of the ways that stewardship and nonprofit organizations go hand in hand.

Deeper, Wider Engagement

Social media gives nonprofits new ways to recognize, showcase and demonstrate accountability of its active supporters. If you are still fighting the use of social media as part of your strategy for nonprofit stewardship, consider that according to Blackbaud, the Internet is a hub of social activity, is 15 times more capable of storing and transmitting information than it was even a few years ago, and that a majority of the U.S. population has high-speed Internet at home.[1] Combine this with the facts that more than 500 million people are using Facebook, there are approximately 50 million Flickr users, approximately 133 million blogs are online, and Twitter gets over 55 million visits per month, and you can soon see how adding social media to your stewardship strategies is highly beneficial to your nonprofit organization. It may even make the difference in whether or not your organization wins out over your competition or keeps your nonprofit doors open for the long haul.

This is not to say that social media will replace the offline methods of stewardship completely, but social media does provide a complementary form of stewardship to your offline methods. Overall, social media is changing the way that nonprofits and donors are interacting. Your donors are using these social media outlets, so the best practice is for your organization to be there or another nonprofit may win them over.

Think of it like this. Your donors, volunteers and even board members are online and using social media networks as a form of communication. When you provide a platform for these conversations that are taking place anyway to take place, then

---

[1] Frank Barry, "Nonprofit Social Media Primer," August, 2009, http://internet.blackbaud.com/atf/cf/%7BA1758E1C-C5FF-4DC3-89ED-DC2343EF76A3%7D/8-09.BBIS.SOCIALMEDIA.WHITEPAPER.PDF

you can become part of the conversation. The ways in which you can use social media as a stewardship tool is only limited by your imagination, but one way to draw inspiration on how you can utilize social media for your own organizational needs may come from seeing how other organizations are putting social media to work.

When the century-old YWCA of San Diego County launched its first interactive social media campaign, complementing the third annual YWCA of San Diego's "Walk a Mile in Her Shoes" event, it was the first time anyone could show their support (even if they weren't able to attend the event in person) in an online forum. The social media campaign invited people to "Declare their intentions to join the fight against domestic violence, donate online, post photos or videos of the shoes they plan to wear during the Walk and share their entries with their friends and family." The two most viral entries were entered to win a donation of $750 and $250 made in their names to the YWCA of San Diego County. Four sweepstakes winners who share an entry with someone else they know were also randomly selected to receive a $50 cash prize or scholarship.

According to Nichole Goodyear, CEO of Brickfish, a performance-based Cost Per Engagement® social media solution that has generated over 300 million consumer engagements and conversations for companies such as QVC, Estee Lauder, Microsoft and Nike, "By adding a social media component to not-for-profit fundraising campaigns and annual events, organizations can heighten awareness and stewardship and generate measurable, viral results." Brickfish was involved in creating the social media campaign for the YWCA of San Diego pro-bono.

Executives from the YWCA and Brickfish highlighted very specific "how-to" stewardship-via-social-media tips for nonprofits such as: (1) Creating a strong theme with clear goals, (2) Identifying and utilizing your best social media assets, (3) Targeting a well-defined audience and (4) Energizing and motivating supporters.

So, how did the third annual YWCA of San Diego's "Walk a Mile in Her Shoes" event and its use of social media as a fundraising tool work out? Even though it rained on the day of the live walk, the social media campaign for the YWCA of San Diego County generated more than 48,000 engagements (the sum of entries, views, reviews and votes) on a national level—this was at a time when the social media campaign would still have another 16 days left to collect donations.

To date, there have been 220 social media campaign entries on a national level; 300 people walked in the "Walk a Mile in Her Shoes" local event; and the social media campaign extended national-level awareness and nearly doubled participation over the previous two years. The YWCA of San Diego County was able to raise $36,000 (as of this point), 90 percent of which was raised online.

Social Bookmarking

The first stop for your social media efforts as part of your stewardship strategies is to include ways that your current donors can add credibility to your organization and your cause by promoting it for you. Social bookmarking websites, such as Digg and StumbleUpon allow your donors to endorse your content or endorse your organization with their own content. When a donor bookmarks your content or their own, the followers they may have or the parties that may be interested in what your nonprofit is doing have a chance to read about it. The stamp of approval from other likeminded people can quickly send the endorsement for your organization all over the web. When your donors are saying that they donate to your organization, it removes the privacy issue from your shoulders because they are the ones out there sharing content on social bookmarking sites.

SNAPSHOP: SPECIAL OLYMPICS

Founded by Eunice Kennedy Shriver, the Special Olympics organization has been championing acceptance and tolerance of people with intellectual disabilities since the inaugural games in 1968. Over the years, Special Olympics has grown from only a few hundred athletes to nearly 3 million in more than 180 countries with different chapters providing year-round coaching, training and competitions for participants. The international organization utilizes social media platforms including Facebook, Twitter and YouTube to inform and educate fans and followers about events and happenings, as well as volunteer opportunities and fundraising efforts within the Special Olympics' global community. In addition, many of the various chapters within the United States, as well as other countries maintain their own social media presence, primarily on Facebook and Twitter.

In March 2009 the Special Olympics organization launched a campaign project to end the use of the derogatory r-word (retard). The campaign, called "Spread the Word to End the Word," implemented several social media tools to effectively "spread the word" of their campaign. A separate website was created for the campaign, as well as a separate Twitter account, Facebook page and YouTube channel, all of which can be accessed from the site's homepage. As of August 2010 the Facebook page accumulated more than 83,500 fans and nearly 5,000 followers on Twitter. Meanwhile, the End the R Word YouTube channel surpassed the Special Olympics channel in channel views, total upload views and subscribers even though it hosted only 22 videos, whereas the Special Olympics channel hosted 90 videos. Posts on Facebook and Twitter drove traffic to the website, where nearly 140,000 people have pledged to stop using the hurtful term, clearly demonstrating social media's power to "spread the word."

Hillary Sinclair, the vice president of business development for Papilia, suggests using social media such as Facebook and Twitter to increase your email base. Sinclair says it should be less of a "get donations" effort and more of an email collection base so that you can then start to communicate with your base to really build your story, giving you the ability to convert them one at a time and more on an individualized basis.

Give them snippets of information, articles your organization is mentioned in or has written, events you're hosting or participating in, volunteer opportunities, or the number of people you have helped through Facebook and Twitter. This can increase your legitimacy so that when you ask potential donors for donations they already know the story of your organization and you have gained their trust in your mission and what you're doing. Sinclair also suggests you use social media in conjunction with your offline efforts in order to maximize the impact.

For example, update Facebook and Twitter the day you send out an appeal, newsletter, or post to your blog. Preferably send your news online and connect that to Twitter and Facebook so they can surf around and make it easy to sign up with your organization through Twitter, Facebook and everywhere else that you can.

Kelly Huff, the vice president of client services for Papilia, shares that there really isn't anything that can compete with building strong, lasting donor relationships en masse than through strategic online touch points. The social media component of the big picture is most effective when layered upon an already successful online platform. Huff says that many of their nonprofit clients have a Facebook and Twitter account because it is expected. Unfortunately, many nonprofits do not have the resources to keep these venues fresh and utilize the platforms to the highest extent, so social media for these nonprofits simply is not working like it should.

Create Raving Fans

While you may provide the platform, such as a Facebook fan page, for your donors to follow the organization, the donors who opt to become fans can highlight themselves as donors, or at the very least supporters of your organization. Many nonprofit organizations are using this to their advantage by even providing an option for donors to make donations directly from the fan page or from a similar social media page. When it is time to roll out the annual fund campaign, announcements can be posted and shared through social media networks as well.

The issue that many nonprofits face is from a stewardship angle—a responsibility exists to ensure that donors are properly recognized and thanked without crossing any privacy lines. Obviously, using a public forum such as social media to say thank you can be a bit on the tricky side.

Some organizations have someone in the nonprofit dedicated to handling the social media networks. Part of this person's responsibility then becomes setting up some kind of "thank you" message campaign. Some thank you messages can be shared with the entire raving fan base that is following you, so a general update using the social media network that thanks all of the donors that have made donations that month or towards the annual fund works here. You can even upload a video thank you for fans to watch and share rather than having to read text.

In addition, you need to implement a system that allows you to thank individuals on a personal level. Even if a donor makes a contribution through a social media outlet, you may not want to thank them personally in a public forum, such as on Facebook, but the thank-you letters you sent in the past may now be thank-you emails instead. Rather than the text-based thank-you email you may have sent even a year ago, now instead you can upload a thank-you video that comes from the representative in the organization.

Better yet, when you have humans or animals involved with the organization's cause or mission, you can drill down to a more personal level by having the person who benefited from the donation provide a thank-you video or present one of the organization representatives with one of the animals that benefited from the fundraising efforts.

Lisa Colton from Darim Online works with nonprofit Jewish organizations, teaching social media training. Lisa says that social media is really powerful for storytelling and for adding value. Will someone sit down for 30 minutes and read your annual report cover to cover? Maybe they will or maybe they will not, but the odds are good that the answer is probably no. Will they read 5 or 10 powerful blog posts, or 30 to 40 tweets over the course of the year to hear your story, feel the impact and get energized and feel part of something? Yes, the odds are likely that they will.

The more value an organization can provide (e.g., When a school uses the expertise of the teachers to teach the parents about the developmental stages of their child), the more likely it is that you will earn someone's attention and then be able to tell your story and build trust that translates into donations.

For all that's new about social media, raising friends and funds is still about relationships. Social media is one tool to help build these relationships. If an organization writes, tweets and updates its Facebook status as a brand and logo, make sure that the real person behind that logo is known. Donors who are going to talk back or comment on a social media page want to know that they are talking to "Suzie" from the 501(c)(3) and not to the 501(c)(3) in general.

As for the power of mentions and saying thank you, Colton says that a donor's voice is very powerful. A "John Smith donated because he ... Won't you...?" is similar to a challenge grant. Even better, it comes straight from the donor. When the message comes directly from the donor, it is a far more compelling message than the voice of the development director, executive director, or director of communications for the organization.

Remember, donors are savvier than ever before. They know when a development director, executive director, or director of communications is simply trying to pull a donation out of them. They are much more likely to take this request from one of their peers and take out their checkbooks than if someone at the organization is asking them for money again.

When Marc Pitman, now a fundraising coach for nonprofit organizations, was the fundraiser at a community hospital, the hospital received a donation of a large amount of stuffed animals. In addition to the normal thank-you letters Marc sent out, he also had pictures taken of him delivering the stuffed animals to patients around the hospital including patients in the clinic, nursery and even the surgical recovery areas. Marc says, "It was great! I posted these to Facebook and emailed them to the donors letting them know I'd publicly thanked them. They loved it! To know their gift was on Facebook made our organization look cutting-edge. And I believe it got our fans to be thinking creatively about supporting the hospital!"

Privacy Issues of Social Media Stewardship

While you want to publicly thank donors, followers and friends on your social media networks, there are privacy issues that organizations need to be aware of before posting in such a public forum. There is a fine line between showing gratitude online to a donor and stepping on his or her privacy rights. A donor may or may not wish for the free world to know that they donated to your organization. While all social media networks have their own privacy policies and terms of use, the organization should also establish its own privacy policy and terms of use.

It may be that you let your donors know upfront that you use social media networks as part of your donation strategy. It may simply be a disclaimer on the social media network profile of the organization or fundraising campaign. You decide what is best for your donors and your organization, but then put it in writing, make sure everyone understands it and abides by it.

You will also need to be aware of the social media network's policy and solicitation laws.

- Understand the privacy policy of the social media outlet you are using. When you put the nonprofit organization on Facebook, Twitter or other social media outlets, you are opening the organization up for copyright and privacy issues. While you can control the messages and information you post to these pages, you may not have as much control over what others post on your pages. Before launching a full-scale social media campaign on any social media outlet, read and fully understand the privacy policy and what controls you do have on these networks. Some outlets allow you to monitor comments before their posting to the public forum, while others do not. It may end up being more damaging than beneficial if people are posting negative comments about the organization and you are not able to control these comments going live or having the ability to remove the ones that do go live.

- Solicitation laws are another issue that arises when nonprofits are asking for donations on social media sites. State laws regulate whether placing a donation button or request on a social media platform triggers the solicitation law. For example, if your donor is in the state of Florida and you have a donation button on a social media outlet, the state of Florida requires you to register with the state under the solicitation law. Since it may not be viable for you to monitor the state laws for each state, what you can do is place a disclaimer on the site that says the organization only accepts donations from the states in which the organization is registered. You can list these states or create a drop-down box on your donation page so the person can choose the state in which they reside before making the donation.

While the donors in your organization proceed through the lifecycle your organization guides them through, one of the primary components of the donation lifecycle is stewardship. Social media networking, marketing and donation acceptance has changed the donation lifecycle because it has introduced new ways for nonprofit organizations to recognize, showcase and demonstrate accountability of its active supporters, donors, volunteers, board members and more.

While the benefits of using social media marketing, sending donation thank-you notes and other stewardship efforts outweigh the drawbacks, organizations do need to be aware of and plan for the potential pitfalls that using social media brings to the nonprofit organizations and to its donors.

It is not about fighting the use of social media as part of your fundraising plans. It is about leveraging the access your organization has to vast social-networking platforms every month. Somewhere in these numbers are large pools of your current and potential donors. The stewardship and accountability you owe to your donors expands into the realm of social media, and you can even recruit donors to help you spread the word and bring in even more donations for your charitable organization.

Since your donors are using these social media outlets in various aspects of their own lives, including philanthropic ones, your nonprofit organization should be using social media too. It adds one more stewardship tool to your donation toolbox and creates at least one more touch point for you to get in front of new donors and keep current supporters fully engaged.

CHAPTER 11

Media and
Public Relations

Your Relationship with the Media Has Changed

SINCE THE TIME OF JULIUS CAESAR, campaigns have needed to establish and protect their presence within public channels of information. Twenty centuries after Caesar's final sound bite, "Et tu, Brute?" public information had become a technological force and industry known as "the media," the fourth estate, with the potential to serve as both advocate and enemy of every person engaged in public-facing causes.

Enter the era of Web 2.0. Per the buzz and punditry perpetuated within social media itself, user-generated content is on the rise, and mainstream media finds itself hustling to find its place. That said, while mainstream media no longer comprise an information oligopoly, the coverage and opinions they convey are still indispensible to charitable organizations across the globe, particularly in the age of ethics, accountability and a sagging economy. And social media is not replacing the mainstream variety; the two are morphing into a new collective mouthpiece for nonprofit organizations.

A study by Chitika Research determined that "news" is the most popular content category for outbound traffic from Twitter and Facebook. Translation: people are spending much of their time sharing and seeking news on these hottest of social media sites. Further translation: good, old-fashioned journalism is the frequent basis of the most coveted kind of social media content, the kind that generates a click to a new destination on the web.

Social media cannot be divorced from mainstream media or from a nonprofit's overall media-relations strategy (yet another reason not to dump social media on the intern and call it a day). As it is redefining the news business, it is redefining the techniques of obtaining favorable coverage. For today's charitable organizations, working with the media requires understanding social media and using it as a reference source, a direct communications tool and a mutual platform with journalists.

Within a social media-driven media relations program, you must:

- Accommodate journalists' use of social media to search out stories
- Maintain a social media dialogue with journalists for pitching, commentary and editorials
- Pitch bloggers in ways that recognize how they emulate and differ from mainstream media journalists
- Monitor social media in determining new messages and pitches
- Issue social media releases in conjunction with standard releases

- Use social media sites for announcements, in conjunction with or in lieu of standard releases
- Build a Web 2.0 media room
- Cultivate user-generated content that mainstream media can incorporate into their own content
- Integrate social media into the crisis-communications process
- Know when to take it offline for those times when social media is not the right tool for media relations

Journalists and Social Media

The intertwining of social media and mainstream media begins with how journalists are employing social media in their work. Studies reveal increasing numbers of media professionals use social media and web resources to research stories, obtain news angles and sources and follow subjects of interest:

- Nearly 70% of journalists are using social networking sites, a 28-percent increase over the previous year (Second Annual Middleberg/SNCR Survey of Media in the Wired World)
- Over 73% of journalists read blogs to stay current on information pertaining to their beats (Bulldog Reporter and TEKGROUP International's 2010 Journalist Survey on Media Relations Practices)
- 73.4% use Facebook to research stories and 55.5% use Twitter (2010 Journalist Survey on Media Relations Practices)

- 54.3% seek audio and video content from corporate websites (2010 Journalist Survey on Media Relations Practices)

"Increasingly, everyone in the business has to use social media," confirms Janet Kornblum, award-winning freelance writer and journalist who specialized in technology and culture as a staff writer for *USA Today* and CNET News. "You have limited time as a journalist."

A charitable organization's social media outreach must be designed with media relations in mind. Journalists will be accessing the same resources as volunteers and supporters to learn about the cause, its accomplishments, its needs and its successes to date. Fortunately, journalists can draw inspiration from information directed toward the public.

"Become an interesting Twitter feed," Kornblum recommends. "Provide lots of useful information. Be prepared to share your information with the opposition to get on their radar screen. Journalists will know you are a good source."

Campaigns should research key journalists' social media presence with tools like MuckRack.com, a Twitter directory for journalists that allows users to find media professionals by Twitter address, beat and geographic location.

"In addition to these tools being valuable for learning about coverage and writing styles, it allows the communication director to build a rapport with journalists," says Alleigh Marré, a Boston-based PR professional, social media strategist and blogger.

Using social media to communicate directly with journalists and track their actions is similar to its use in other relationships. Following journalists on Twitter, friending them on Facebook and connecting with them on LinkedIn are all acceptable practices.

They should return the favor, as it will help them cover their beats related to your cause. Like other social media associations, do not abuse the conduit with excessive communications.

Pay attention to what journalists are saying in their general social media posts. If they are looking for information or quotes on a particular subject, they are likely to announce it through social media. Respond quickly to such requests by offering background information, interview subjects and relevant organizational and user-generated content such as photos and video. If they contact you through a direct Twitter, Facebook or LinkedIn message, respond as soon as possible.

Social bookmarking is another platform with media relations value. Sites such as delicious.com and Diigo.com allow users to create archives of web content. A campaign can curate an online library of third-party articles, studies, videos and charts that support the organization's positions and reinforce its position in the context of larger issues, or as a standalone piece. Users can network within social bookmarking sites and share information, creating another chance to connect with journalists and make their jobs easier by providing background material.

Blogger Relations

Blogs are a cornerstone of social media, representing one of the earliest and most visible forms of user-generated content. It is difficult to overstate blogs' influence on nonprofit organizations—or any organizations—as a 24/7 outlet for independent commentary, a repeater station for mainstream media coverage and a digital hub for volunteers and donors. Nonprofit organizations may feel as though social media has suddenly descended upon them and they are not quite prepared, but blogs have been a crucial part of communications strategy for years. A December 2003 article from Associated Press describes the presidential campaign of Gen. Wesley Clark enlisting the talents of blogging pioneer Cameron Barrett to combat "Internet-powered front-runner Howard Dean." Imagine what a strong blogger could do for your organization.

Important to remember is that new blogs can arise literally overnight to affect an organization's cause, particularly at the local and regional levels. Every blog must be considered through the same set of media-relations rules, a protocol unique to bloggers that accommodates both their similarities and differences when compared to traditional journalists. If you are not yet certain your organization can support its own blog, it's best to begin by seeking to become a guest blogger on a blog that is already well-trafficked and relevant to your cause.

Deciding which blogs matter can be accomplished through a combination of basic observations and more sophisticated measurements. In smaller causes, blogs will reveal their relevance simply by commenting on the mission, the need and the progress being made. Such blogs may be affiliated with local traditional media and may be immediately identifiable. Others can be located using a Google Blogs search of keywords pertaining to causes like yours. For larger organizations, blogs can be prioritized by their web metrics for traffic and/or influence as measured by sites such as Alexa, Technorati and BlogPulse.com.

Blogging experts like Jason Vines, author of the blog "Social Media Explorer," and Deirdre Breakenridge, principal of Mango! Marketing, recommend immersion in blogs of consequence. Follow them. Read past posts. Begin commenting on posts. Responses from the organization or those who have benefitted will show the blogger and the blog's followers that you are paying attention and find the blog important, even if it is at odds with your cause's position. It also enters your organization into the conversation, which is the essence of every influential blog. There is no guarantee that comments from your organization will be made public, but an astute blogger will not filter them.

Direct contact with bloggers can occur through a number of means. Media database services such as Cision will have contact information for more prominent bloggers and mainstream media journalists who blog. Many blogs will have an email link to the blogger or a contact form on the "about" page. Charitable organizations can also follow bloggers on Twitter and send them direct messages when they in turn follow the cause. Pithy and personalized communications tend to rule in the blogosphere. In her book *The New Community Rules: Marketing on the Social Web*, social media consultant and author Tamar Weinberg warns against using standard press releases in reaching out to bloggers. In-depth information should be held in reserve until after a blogger responds to a short pitch.

Knowing a blog's tone and prior content will dictate pitches and follow-ups. Supportive blogs can receive more frequent and detailed information with greater likelihood that it will be used for content. Examine such blogs' readership and image. A blog that supports your cause but spews invective and makes wild charges about causes similar to yours can harm your institutional image. Choose your friends in the blogosphere fairly but wisely. Care should also be taken when sending written pitches. Darren Rowse, founder of Problogger.net, warns that any information sent may end up verbatim in a post due to the web's copy-and-paste culture and a freewheeling spirit among certain bloggers.

Blogs can be potent channels for exclusive information. Special interviews with the leadership or spokesperson of a cause (particularly when this is a well-known celebrity or public figure) or major announcements delivered through carefully chosen blogs can reach constituents quickly and spark more mainstream media coverage as they vie to break the news to their audiences.

"Bloggers are generally much more accessible, much more willing to write," says Adam Haverstock, communications consultant. When distributing news, he often goes first to bloggers with the eventual goal of driving mainstream media coverage. "They'll write on it immediately; then it will come out in print."

Blogs can develop stories that are important to your organization's cause, but receive insufficient coverage in traditional outlets. Active bloggers are eager for scoops to burnish their newsmaker credentials. Blogs also present more than the written word. Multimedia content such as web video and podcasts should be pushed to blogs or developed in cooperation with bloggers (see "User-Generated Content" later in this chapter).

Monitoring Social Media

Every social media program requires a monitoring strategy. It is the Web 2.0 equivalent of the surveys and focus groups that nonprofit organizations have used for decades. Social media monitoring directly affects media relations with your organization by gauging:

- The most frequently discussed topics relating to your cause, allowing the campaign to tailor media pitches and public communications accordingly

- The most frequently shared news stories, allowing your cause to focus on the journalists and outlets exerting the

> most influence among people discussing the topic via social media

Social media monitoring is easily accomplished—perhaps too easily as there are a large number of tools, platforms and sites that can track the online conversation. Allocation of resources and focus on essential outcomes are key.

"There are over 100 social media monitoring tools to review so it's prudent to clearly define your campaign goals for what you want to measure and the downstream actions you want to take," recommends Cathy McCall, principal of Hamilton Hill Associates, a digital marketing and strategy company based in Denver.

Like popular social media platforms themselves, many social media monitoring tools are free. Google's "Updates" search (found under the "more" tab on the Google search bar) monitors Twitter mentions of search terms with a graph for mention frequency and the ability to track past occurrences of the term. The self-explanatory Twitter Search and Facebook Search plumb those respective platforms. Twitter's search engine, mentioned previously (www.search.twitter.com), can send notices of keyword occurrences through an RSS feed. The Google Blogs search function reveals keywords occurring within individual blogs as do blog search engines such as Technorati and BlogPulse.com. Google Alerts can send notices of keyword appearances in blogs as can RSS feeds from sites like Technorati.

Paid services can provide more sophisticated social media monitoring. Trackur.com allows users to follow many different social media channels and view results in a unified format. It can determine the influence of specific posts and content by measuring incoming links and traffic. Radian6 tracks a vast array of social media, providing analytics on traffic and influence. Pricing for such services can range from approximately $20 per month for Trackur's basic service to $500 per month for Radian6's entry point. A charitable organization's size and budget will quickly determine whether it should go the free or paid route with social media monitoring, but for the most part nonprofits do just fine with the freeware, as their own internal tracking systems (e.g., donor databases, email tracking) can help to tell them the rest of the story.

Social media monitoring to support media relations parallels an organization's overall tracking of channels and sites. The methodology is similar to SEO techniques to gather paid search and organic search results. It comes down to keywords: top names associated with your cause, issues, taglines and geography (such as activity within a region). Qualities (e.g., "champion for the homeless," "relentless on literacy for all Americans") can also be part of the search matrix if the terms are hot buttons. Specific headlines, journalists and outlets should also be part of the ongoing search to measure their popularity and influence. Maintain a spreadsheet to track keyword occurrence, organized by trends and topics. Many paid monitoring services will automate such reports.

"Your team will want to develop a prioritization model that guides the timing and action taken from social media trends," advises Cathy McCall. "Watch for frequency, popularity and passion as the key criteria in your model."

Social media monitoring results should guide media pitches and releases. Upon recognizing a positive trend for the nonprofit or the industry in which it operates, an organization's media relations team can recommend new stories to substantiate it. Negative trends can be fought through the same methods (e.g., the current downward trend in giving across the board). Determining the popularity of specific news features focuses an organization on journalists and outlets wielding the most influence. This can be done by tracking social media mentions and links and by checking the popularity measurements for stories ("most read," "most shared," "most liked") found on media websites.

"We always seek out authors of pieces getting a lot of play," says Rachel Dodsworth, principal of Adsworth Media. "We make sure to continuously push articles from the local media in order to further build relationships."

Through media monitoring and supporter connection, Dodsworth guides supporters to retweet and share positive stories, ultimately encouraging the journalists and outlets responsible to produce similar coverage to maintain traffic and readership. The same tactics hold true across nonprofit organizations. This is not an effort to slant journalism; it is a means to reinforce public response to certain types of coverage. In short, the media wants to produce stories that interest the public.

Your Media Release

The Social Media Press Release

Releasing the news in the social media era requires a blend of new and old methods, beginning with a Web 2.0 version of a PR staple. The social media press release (SMPR) is an evolved form of the standard press release, incorporating the tools and the tone of Web 2.0. Todd Defren, principal of Shift Communications, is credited with creating the first template for the social media release in 2006.

The social media press release differs from a standard release through its brevity, sharable nature and links to supporting online content—all hallmarks of social media itself. Per the Defren template, which has been modified since its inception and is being continually adapted by its users, the social media release reduces verbiage while emphasizing the means to share its information and to view related content. It is placed on the Web with a unique URL and "distributed" though its links and sharing tools, not by a wire service or e-blast. Contact information and a headline comprise the beginning of the release. Beneath the headline, a bulleted list of facts can suffice for the copy. From a writing perspective, gone are the days of "writing for AP." This has been replaced by "writing for SEO" or keeping keywords and search top of mind while creating intriguing and informative press release content.

The social media release links to a social bookmarking page. A charitable organization can use this feature to juxtapose the release with independent articles and commentary that validate the organization's relevant positions and accomplishments.

Quotes are broken out in a separate section apart from the main copy. Defren recommends up to two quotes per individual with additional quotes available for outlets seeking exclusive information. Per the push for authenticity in social media, keep the quotes short and free of jargon and slogans.

The left sidebar of the social media release presents links to supporting multimedia content: images, podcasts/MP3 files and video. The right sidebar contains moderated comments regarding the release and a blogroll of sites that link to the organization's news. These last two elements embody social media's mandate for dialogue and transparency. They may seem edgy to many nonprofits and an invitation for negative remarks. Properly managed, comments and blogger links will show the organization's connectedness and willingness to publicly back its position on mission-central issues. This openness and courage of conviction, particularly within those organizations faced with controversial causes, will not be lost on perceptive journalists.

The footer of the social media release contains sharing tools such as an RSS feed, a "Share This" universal bookmark widget and tags for Technorati. These tools make it easier for journalists to find and follow the organization's releases. The general public can benefit as well from such social media accessibility. Per social media experts such as David Meerman Scott, Brian Solis and Deirdre Breakenridge, releases are no longer just for the media; they are communications for all publics.

The Standard Press Release

The standard press release is not "dead," as is often speculated. It should be written with the concise sensibilities of Web 2.0—no rambling, posturing or stilted quotes. A traditional release is a good vehicle for a more "narrative" approach to the main copy, written in a customary article style. It is also the center of the classic "push" strategy of media relations, sending information to the media via the wire or email. A standard release should have a link to a corresponding social media release. This "doubling up" is perfectly acceptable as making information available through multiple channels has always been a sound media relations strategy.

Be sensitive to the preferred contact methods of journalists covering smaller-scale causes. You may be waging a campaign in an area where global, charitable-organization coverage is in the hands of an exclusive group of writers and editors who insist on more traditional forms of communication.

Social Media Posts

Organizations commonly use Facebook, Twitter and other social media platforms to post news and announcements. Charitable organizations should use this basic tactic as well. The intent is to increase opportunities to capture key audiences' attention quickly, give them the equivalent of a sound bite via the post (this premise is built into Twitter's 140-character limit) and link them to more detailed information. Using social media to push releases and announcements simultaneously notifies journalists and the public. If an item is truly newsworthy, the media know that word is out, compelling them to generate in-depth coverage and provide value to an aware audience.

Social media news posts can enhance the organization's website, driving traffic to the site and help keep its content fresh.

Posting to social media sites can eliminate the need for many typical releases, namely those that call attention to positive media coverage or favorable mentions. A quick tweet or Facebook message directing viewers to the source content saves the effort and potential message-dilution of a release to note a fundraising campaign "win" in the form of a leadership gift.

"We don't need to write a press release if the media is telling the story we want," concludes Dodsworth.

The Web 2.0 Media Room

An online media room has been a communications requirement since the 1990s. A Web 2.0 media room enhances the concept using social media techniques, allowing journalists to access information more consistently and efficiently. Todd Defren is also the early proponent of the Web 2.0 media room, introducing a template on his blog in 2007.

Defren and Lee Odden, founder of TopRank Online Marketing, both encourage the use of blog software and typical blog features in constructing a Web 2.0 media room. Odden cites blog software's content-management capabilities, SEO enhancements and automatic RSS features as the means to make an online media room's content simpler to locate within the site and easier to find when conducting web searches.

Defren uses blog site structure liberally in his social media newsroom template, which like his social media release template is crowdsourced (a design derived from others' feedback and experiences) and opensourced (given freely to the online world in hopes the concept will spread). In adapting Defren's corporate-oriented template to charitable organizations, the upper left-hand corner contains the organization's basic information including a link to its LinkedIn profile. Links and contact information for an organization's media contacts occupies the top right-hand corner. A search window prominently displayed at the top of the page will allow journalists and other viewers to find content by keyword.

Archives for media coverage and news releases dominate the center of the newsroom page. Each post features an abstract and a link to the complete piece along with sharing tools for emailing and social bookmarking. Both the media coverage and news release sections allow visitors to opt for updates by RSS feed or email. For in-demand interviews with experts associated with your organization, offer an easy-to-use interview request form that might take only seconds to complete. Be sure that responses are handled promptly or the beauty of this convenience will be lost, particularly for journalists on tight deadlines needing an expert fast.

The schedule section occupies the bottom center of the page. Social media tools can be used to document "time and place" for the organization's leadership. Alleigh Marré recommends the use of foursquare to display an organization's whereabouts, whether it's a standard event, an interview, or an informal gathering with volunteers (note: updates are voluntarily entered). Foursquare posts can be synced to Twitter and Facebook, allowing the media and the public to track the organization easily.

Defren's template also includes a multimedia gallery with links to images and videos, a social bookmarking section and a tag cloud. This last component allows visitors to search for content by keyword, with the most commonly occurring terms appearing in a larger font to indicate their frequency and importance. The "blog-like" feature helps the media determine at a glance which topics are emphasized in the organization's content.

SNAPSHOT: MARQUETTE UNIVERSITY

It has long been regarded as easier and more effective to learn a foreign language when you are living or studying abroad in the country where that language is the native tongue. Using this principle, foreign language professors have integrated the use of Skype webcasts into their foreign language classes at Marquette University in Milwaukee, Wisconsin, enabling students to have one-on-one conversation time with native speakers who are also studying English as a foreign language in their universities.

Students simply go to the foreign language lab and split time with English-learning students at South American universities who are also participating in the program. Utilizing Skype and actuating real-life conversations has been paramount to many students' learning experience. Oftentimes teachers do not have the time or resources to provide students with one-on-one attention, but with the foreign language exchange program students are giving and receiving private tutoring sessions. In a 2007 article for *Christian Science Monitor* one student revealed that his Skype conversations have helped his Spanish improve more than the traditional classroom lessons, adding, "I feel more comfortable speaking in class than I did before."[1]

Many students utilize other social media platforms to stay in touch with their foreign language pen pals beyond the classroom. An astounding 85.3 percent of Marquette University's Spanish language Professor Janet Banhidi's students maintain communication with their South American Skype classmates through Facebook. One student added, "In the end, the best part of this exchange was gaining a friend who I still today talk with on Facebook."[2]

[1] Matthew Rusling, "Learn a foreign language—over the Web," *Christian Science Monitor*, August 16, 2007, http://www.csmonitor.com/2007/0816/p13s02-legn.html

[2] Greg Ferenstein, "3 Ways Educators Are Embracing Social Technology," Mashable, January 10, 2010, http://mashable.com/2010/01/10/educators-social-technology/

User-Generated Content

Social media is user-generated content—written word, audio, photos, video, multimedia. Nonprofit campaigns can spawn copious amounts from engaged volunteers and supporters, and mainstream media is increasingly embracing this content both as a source of story leads and as content directly presented to its audiences, per CNN.com's iReport.

"You definitely want to create as much user-generated content as possible," recommends Adam Haverstock.

A nonprofit organization should post basic guidelines on creating and presenting user-generated content, including tips on:

- Writing blog posts and social news articles including tone, length and how to develop a topic.
- Videography and photography including subject selection, basic composition and easy lighting techniques.
- Recording podcasts including use of basic recording equipment (most laptops have built-in microphones), writing scripts and conducting interviews.

- Uploading finished content to the campaign's channels and pages on sites like YouTube, Flickr and MyPodcast. com.
- Sharing finished content using social media sites.

Keep the advice simple and fun. Remind supporters that the organization doesn't want slick or canned materials, that authenticity and "the volunteers' voices" are the most important aspects. Helping supporters create user-generated content is the Web 2.0 version of guiding them in writing letters to the editor (still an important function itself).

Pitching journalists on user-generated content requires tact. "Let things be organic," says Janet Kornblum. "It's fine to start a conversation and then suggest that journalists check something out, but expect that if they find anything quotable or interesting they may want to contact the person who said it."

Social Media and Crisis Management

Every charitable organization needs to operate as if it is in crisis mode even if nothing bad is happening. In other words, growing a pool of supporters is an all-the-time task so that when crisis does strike, your organization will have a core of believers ready to stand by the cause and vouch for your organization's good name. Social media provides a new opportunity to anticipate and counteract crises, but it must be used judiciously and integrated with overall communications strategy.

Brian Solis blogs that the social web has transformed crisis communications from a reactive discipline to a proactive one of "listening, observing and participating."

Social media serves as an intelligence gatherer because it is where people learn about and share negative news, be it media coverage or user-generated content.

"You can't call something a non-issue and hope it goes away," Dodsworth explains. "Social media will tell you if you have an issue or not."

While a crisis will doom complacency, it's also not an occasion for kneejerk reactions, which can be all-too-easily transmitted through social media. Eric Anderson says, "The most important thing is to get the response right the first time, even if that takes a little longer. It's very difficult to undo the damage caused by starting off on the wrong foot."

Social media must work in concert with other communication tools. Once the crisis response moves forward, it may be the first means of communication an organization chooses, its very use conveying a subtext of immediacy, openness and technological savvy. When the time is right for that communication, one additional advantage of a social media response is the insertion of the organization's message directly into the online dialogue, allowing it to be observed and shared straight from the source.

Although known for immediacy and authenticity, social media can become a barrier against mainstream media—deliberately or inadvertently. In a crisis, the organization's spokesperson cannot say his or her piece via social media and declare the matter closed. Any initial statements, from a tweet to a video address posted on YouTube, must be considered an invitation for journalists' follow-up. It is acceptable to counter negative issues in organizationally generated content, but be prepared to respond promptly to media inquiries and to take questions.

When to Take It Offline

While social media can greatly increase the effectiveness of media relations, it is not a blanket solution. There are times when you need to take a conversation with the media offline to effectively transmit certain information and nurture journalist relationships.

Exclusives that give one outlet a head start over others require a personal touch. Standard rules about awarding exclusives still apply:

- Is the recipient of the story the best communication channel for the organization?
- Does the recipient warrant the special treatment?
- Will you irreparably harm relationships with other media over the favoritism?

Potentially negative or damaging information should also be addressed face-to-face. The sensitivity of such issues calls for direct communication, which will also allow both the organization and media side to interpret intent and meaning, qualities than cannot be conveyed nearly as well in electronic communication, especially in the typical shorthand of social media.

Running disagreements with the media should not be played out in social media. A posted rebuttal to an unfavorable piece can dissolve into a tweet war or its equivalent on other platforms. It used to be said that it was unwise to pick a fight with someone who buys ink by the barrel, meaning traditional media always had the last word due to their resources and control of communication. It may be tempting to think that has changed with Web 2.0 now that everyone has the same number of pixels; however, user-generated venting can wound an organization's core positioning.

The signature issue of authenticity can dictate when social media is not the solution. "I don't like the idea of credible news sources quoting Twitter or Facebook without fact-checking," says Adam Haverstock. "How many accounts get hacked every day?"

In the end, there is no program or web dashboard to tell you when to step away from social media and engage in a direct conversation. There are only the instincts and experience borne of able organizational communications management.

Social media is not a goal unto itself. It is not a magical replacement for the traditional, independent public channels of information that have covered the work of charitable organizations. As it is for other crucial actions—organizing volunteers, raising funds and creating ongoing engagement opportunities—social media is a tool for working with the mainstream media. Successful charitable organizations will seize this and the attendant opportunities.

CHAPTER 12

The Ongoing Cycle
of Giving

WHEN WE CONSIDER THE rich arsenal of tools at our disposal for engaging, cultivating, soliciting and stewarding supporters, volunteers, boards of directors and others, social media offers the perfect model for what nonprofit and charitable organizations strive to do: Start a conversation with their base of support and then continue that conversation not only through the next event or board meeting or fundraising campaign, but through a lifetime.

Like the hiring process, or new customer acquisition, we know that it is much more difficult—and much more costly to acquire and train a new employee, or to sell a new customer on trying our product or service. Therefore, finding new ways to create "supporters for life" related to your cause is the optimal scenario. Social media success rises and falls based on this ongoing engagement, making these online channels the ideal vehicles for achieving long-term relationship building.

We must keep in mind that while you must avoid taking the "next shiny object" approach to the channels you create, you must pay close attention to how your base of support continues to evolve, be it in terms of the social networking platforms they are using more (or less), or the technologies they are most closely aligned with (e.g., mobile devices, laptops, iPods or iPads, e-readers).

The most important piece of advice for anyone working within the nonprofit world is that you must shape your communications strategies not on platforms or networks that you do not control, but on value-added content, so that when you find your audiences moving from Twitter to Twitter-plus, or from Friendster and MySpace to the next iteration of a Facebook network, you will be prepared to move seamlessly and nimbly with an eye toward sustaining the engagement while remaining top of mind as the organization of choice in a sea of worthy causes.

You must compete not only on the core of your missions, but also on your abilities to travel and grow with your core of supporters, while considering the needs of the next generation of supporters. Most of what you do in the nonprofit sector is about connecting in the short-term for long-term, multi-generational effect.

Social media provides the ideal mix of tools for accomplishing beyond the must-do's and driving you into engagements you may once have considered beyond your reach. This enables you to break free of the almost universal concerns from supporters such as, "You only contact us when you want our money," or "Every time I turn around, Organization X is asking me for something else." Volunteer and donor fatigue are real and growing concerns for any nonprofit, hence social media accomplishes the task of opening up new and ongoing opportunities for support from new pipelines of individuals who might be willing to engage.

We are in the midst of an exciting sea change in the ways in which we build relationships with core constituencies, and while we haven't yet landed, we have amassed sufficient data to know that (a) even as it continues to evolve, social media is here to stay; (b) while philanthropic dollars continue to shrink in a sagging economy, never before have charitable organizations had such unbridled access to existing and new target groups; and (c) sitting on the sidelines is no longer acceptable for any organization, in that you risk becoming invisible at best and at worst, irrelevant.

The goal for any nonprofit or charitable organization is to use the content presented here as a launching pad for beginning or growing your social media strategy. Remember that this strategy must be incorporated into your more longstanding marketing and communications efforts (e.g., direct mail, phon-a-thons), and you must always maintain an iterative approach through listening to your constituents and then pouring these learnings back into your efforts.

For those who feel they have missed the social-media train, there is always another train, and starting now means taking advantage of the best practices that have been shaped by colleagues and competitors. No organization can afford to take a pass, and each entity will bring its own level of creativity and understanding to the process of shaping a sound social media plan for the purpose of growing a worthy cause.

I wish you the very best of luck in your efforts to advance your organization's mission through some of the most dynamic and powerful relationship-building strategies the nonprofit sector has ever seen, and in the spirit of social media, I encourage you to share your experiences with me. You can do so by sending an email to contact@socialmediasurvivalguide.com. I would love to hear from you and welcome the opportunity to help share your story with others in an upcoming publication.

BONUS ONLINE EXTRAS

Access more great tips for
your online fundraising success:

Getting Started: Five Steps to Launching
Your Social Media Fundraising Campaign

How to Write an Effective
Online Fundraising Appeal

Visit www.SocialMediaForNonprofitsBook.com

The Social Media Survival Guide Series

Just as organizations and individuals are eager to embrace the opportunity, they are hesitant to take on additional risk, leaving many to fall behind the competition in the wake of uncertainty. **The Social Media Survival Guide** and its companion titles are designed to make social media accessible, tactical and easy to use right away. **The Survival Guide** series will help you to market successfully within this space, maintain a competitive edge and boost results—from increasing sales, to landing the job, to winning elections.

The Social Media Survival Guide:
Everything You Need to Know to Grow Your Business Exponentially with Social Media

The Social Media Survival Guide (Spanish-language edition)

The Online Job Search Survival Guide:
Everything You Need to Know to Use Social Networking to Land a Job Now

The Social Media Survival Guide for Political Campaigns:
Everything You Need to Know to Get Your Candidate Elected Using Social Media

The Social Media Survival Guide for Nonprofit and Charitable Organizations: How to Build Your Base of Support and Fast-Track Your Fundraising Efforts with Social Media

Order at SocialMediaSurvivalGuide.com

.

Manufactured By: RR Donnelley
Breinigsville, PA USA
February, 2011

.